The Contemporary
Quest for Jesus

FACETS

The Contemporary Quest for Jesus

N. T. Wright

Fortress Press
Minneapolis

THE CONTEMPORARY QUEST FOR JESUS

Facets edition 2002

This volume is an excerpt from: N. T. Wright, *Jesus and the Victory of God* (London: SPCK; Minneapolis: Fortress Press, 1996).

Cover and book design: Joseph Bonyata
Cover graphic: copyright © nonstøck inc.
Used by permission.

0-8006-3482-9

The paper used in this publication meets the minimum requirements of American National Standard for Information Sciences—Permanence of Paper for Printed Library Materials, ANSI Z329.48-1984.

Manufactured in the U.S.A.

06   05   04   03   02   1   2   3   4   5   6   7   8   9   10

Contents

1
The "Quests" and Their Usefulness

Jesus through History

Since Albert Schweitzer, it has been customary to think that the "Quest of the Historical Jesus" began with Hermann Samuel Reimarus in the eighteenth century. There is some truth in that. But quite a long time before Reimarus, and at least as important in the overall history of the subject, is the work and the theological position of the sixteenth-century reformers. Despite their desire for a church based on "scripture alone," and their insistence on the literal sense of those scriptures, it may be questioned whether they ever found a satisfactory way of making the literal sense of the *Gospels* yield worthwhile theological results. If what one needed was clear, "timeless" doctrinal and ethical teaching, one must go (so it seemed) to the Epistles. The Gospels must then be turned into repositories of the same "timeless truth." This was achieved by treating them, not literally, as stories which were there for their own sake, but as collections of sayings of Jesus which then became, as it were, mini-epistles; or of events which showed the clash between false religion (here represented by sixteenth-century legalists or formalists thinly disguised as Pharisees) and the true one offered by Jesus. All this culminates, of course, in the event to which the Gospels really do point, the death and resurrection of Jesus. This event is to be understood not as the execution of an awkward figure who refused to stop rocking the first-century Jewish or Roman boat, but as the saving divine act whereby the sins of the world were dealt with once and for all.

This divine act, however, did not have very much to do with what went before. The fact that the Gospels reached their climax with the death of Jesus seemed to have little to do with any significance to be drawn from his life, except that the conflict he engendered by preaching about love and grace was the proximate reason for his death, which the redeemer God then "counted" in a redemptive scheme which had nothing to do with that historical reason. The reformers had very thorough answers to the question: "Why did Jesus die?" They did not have nearly such good answers to the question: "Why did Jesus live?" Their successors to this day have not often done any better. But the question will not go away. If the only available answer is "to give some shrewd moral teaching, to live an exemplary life, and to prepare for sacrificial death," we may be forgiven for thinking it a little lame. It also seems, as we shall see, quite untrue to Jesus' own understanding of his vocation and work.

It would not, then, be much of a caricature to say that orthodoxy, as represented by much popular preaching and writing, has had no clear idea of the purpose of Jesus' ministry. For many conservative theologians it would have been sufficient if Jesus had been born of a virgin (at any time in human history, and perhaps from any race), lived a sinless life, died a sacrificial death, and risen again three days later. (In some instances the main significance of this would be the conclusion: the Bible is all true.) The fact that, in the midst of these events, Jesus actually said and did certain things, which included giving wonderful moral teaching and annoying some of his contemporaries, functions within this sort of orthodox scheme merely as a convenience. Jesus becomes a composite figure, a cross between Socrates defeating the Sophists and Luther standing up against the Papists. His ministry and his death are thus loosely connected. The force of this is lost, though, when the matter is thought through. If the main purpose of Jesus' ministry was to die on the cross, as the outworking of an abstracted atonement-theology, it starts to look as though he simply took on the establishment in order to get himself crucified, so that the abstract sacrificial theology could be put into effect. This makes both ministry and death look like sheer contrivance.

For the same reasons, as we have already suggested, the reformers and their successors have seemed to be much better exponents of the Epistles than of the Gospels. Although Luther and the others did their best to grasp the meaning of (say) Galatians as a whole, and to relate it to their contemporary setting, little attempt was made to treat (say) Matthew in the same way, or to ask what the evangelists thought they were doing in not merely collecting interesting and useful material about Jesus but actually stringing it together in what looks for all the world like a continuous narrative, a story. My later argument will, I hope, indicate that these two weaknesses—the failure to ask about the theological significance of the ministry of Jesus, and the failure to treat the Gospels with full seriousness as they stand, that is, as *stories*— are among the chief causes of much present confusion, and that they can and must be remedied.

The reformers, then, focused not on the Jesus of history for his own sake, but on the results, the "benefits," of his work. "This is to know Christ, to know his benefits . . . unless one knows why Christ took upon himself human flesh and was crucified, what advantage would accrue from having learned his life's history?" (Philipp Melanchthon). Though this does not exactly say that one cannot or must not "learn his life's history," it certainly directs attention away from it, and towards an abstract—and therefore, it seems, a more easily applicable—doctrine of incarnation and atonement. The emphasis on the *pro me* ("for me") of the gospel seemed to be threatened by the specificity, the historical unrepeatableness, of the Gospels. Some of the reformers, at least, intended, and all effected, a break with history: they founded essentially new churches, in supposed continuity with Christ and the apostles (and perhaps the Fathers), but in decided discontinuity with the medieval church. Along with this there came about, at least in principle, another break with history, this time at the very heart of the faith.

Continuity with Christ meant sitting loose to the actuality of Jesus, to his Jewishness, to his own aims and objectives. This is not the place to explore why the reformers made the moves they did, nor have I the competence for such an inquiry. Suffice it to note here that the claim of later Lutherans such as Kähler and Bultmann to be standing in the Reformation tradition when they put forward the "historic, biblical Christ" over against the "so-called historical Jesus," or when they stripped away the layers of Jewish apocalyptic mythology to uncover the timeless call to decision, has solid ground under its feet. There may also be a disquieting note: a hint of the theologian spurning the historian, of the elder brother rejecting the rehabilitated prodigal.

Within post-Reformation circles, both Catholic and Protestant, there has been a general use of the Gospels as sourcebooks for ethics and doctrine, for edifying tales or, smuggled in behind the back of the *sensus literalis* ("literal sense"), allegory. What else was there to do with them? Attention was directed elsewhere: to the creation of "Christian" societies, and their maintenance and defense by argument and war; to the burning theological and practical issues of the day. For the church, which one way or another still held much of Europe in its control, Jesus was the divine Christ who redeemed the world and whose derivative authority, whether through pope or preacher, was exercised to the supposed benefit of that world. The icon was in place, and nobody asked whether the Christ it portrayed—and in whose name so much good and ill was done—was at all like the Jesus whom it claimed to represent. Nobody, that is, until Reimarus.

The hypothesis I shall propose shares the reformers' concern for theology, but not their uncertainty about the value of the history of Jesus' life in relation to the theological and hermeneutical task. From that point of view I cannot but welcome the rise of the critical movement, which drew the attention of the Reformation churches to that history which had, for two centuries at least, been conveniently ignored.

The Rise of the Critical Movement: From Reimarus to Schweitzer

Hermann Samuel Reimarus (1694–1768) was the great iconoclast. His *Fragments* (published posthumously by G. E. Lessing in 1778) do not constitute the greatest of the "Lives of Jesus" chronicled by Schweitzer, but he usually gets the credit for being the first to challenge the ruling myth, or at least the first whose challenge was heard. As Colin Brown has recently shown, Reimarus himself must be seen in the light of English Deism, which created a favorable climate for the questioning upon which he embarked. He was not writing in, or to, a vacuum. He was, on the contrary, reacting sharply to the mainline tradition of his day. That tradition—of European Christianity, and particularly continental Protestantism—had its own view of Jesus and the Gospels, and Reimarus was determined to prove it wrong. His aim seems to have been to destroy Christianity (as he knew it) at its root, by showing that it rested on historical distortion or fantasy. Jesus was a Jewish reformer who became increasingly fanatical and politicized; and he failed. His cry of dereliction on the cross signaled the end of his expectation that his God would act to support him. The disciples fell back on a different model of Messiahship, announced that he had been "raised," and waited for their God to bring the end of the world. They too were disappointed, but instead of crying out in despair they founded the early Catholic church, which to Reimarus may have looked like much the same thing. The thesis is devastatingly simple. History leads away from theology. Cash out the ancestral inheritance, and you will end up feeding the pigs. Jesus was no more than a Jewish revolutionary; the gospel hushed this up in the interests of the new religion. Go back to the beginning, and you will find your faith (and the European way of life which was based on it) resting on a failed Messiah and a fraudulent gospel. The "Quest" began as an explicitly anti-theological, anti-Christian, anti-dogmatic movement. Its initial agenda was *not* to find a Jesus upon whom Christian faith might be based, but to show that the faith of the church (as it was then conceived) could not in fact be based on the real Jesus of Nazareth.

We should be clear that the post-Reformation church had laid itself wide open to this attack. Reimarus was simply exploiting the split between history and faith implicit in the emphasis of Melanchthon's dictum, quoted above. He claimed that the Gospels were records of early Christian faith, not transcripts of history, and that when we study the actual history we discover a very different picture. It simply will not do to say that such a question ought not even to be raised. Schweitzer's objection to Reimarus was that he should not have thought of Jesus' eschatology in a purely political sense, though he was right to emphasize Jesus' claim that the hope of Israel was about to be fulfilled. My own objection would be similar, only wider: Jesus did not support the Jewish national resistance to Rome, but rather opposed it. But Jesus must certainly be understood within his own historical context. In so far as the reformers and their successors did not understand him thus, Reimarus, or somebody like him, must be seen, not just as a protester against Christianity, but— despite his intentions—as a true reformer of it. This is not to side with Reimarus and other Enlightenment thinkers against Christian ortho- doxy; it is to acknowledge that the challenge of the Enlightenment might, despite itself, benefit Christianity as well as threatening it. The elder brother had better not be too snooty if and when the prodigal returns.

Let us be clear. People often think that the early "lives of Jesus" were attempting to bring the church back to historical reality. They were not. They were attempting to show what historical reality really was, in order that, having glimpsed this unattractive sight, people might turn away from orthodox theology and discover a new free- dom. One looked at the history in order then to look elsewhere, to the other side of Gotthold Ephraim Lessing's "ugly ditch," to the eternal truths of reason unsullied by the contingent facts of everyday events, even extraordinary ones like those of Jesus. The fascinating thing, looking back two hundred years later, is that the appeal to his- tory against itself, as it were, has failed. History has shown itself to contain more than the idealists believed it could. It is in this sense that Reimarus was, despite himself, a genuine reformer of the faith. He pulled back the curtain, thinking to expose the poverty of Christian origins. But the invitation to look more closely, once issued, could not be withdrawn; and within the unpromising historical specificity of the story of Jesus we can now, I believe, discern after all the buried treasure of the gospel. We may have to sell all—not least Lessing's metaphysic—in order to be able to buy it. But the one thing we cannot do is to tug the veil back into place. Reimarus has, it seems, done us a great service. His historical approach may have had its faults, but the fault may ultimately be a happy one.

The same could not be said of all those who came between Reimarus and Schweitzer. Their story is well enough known, and often enough told, to need little elaboration here. The famous *Life of Jesus Critically Examined* of David Friedrich Strauss (1835) tried to bring Christianity into line with rationalism and with speculative Hegelian philosophy, ruling out the miraculous by means of an *a priori* (and having no difficulty in showing that many of the orthodox rationalizations of miracles were simply laughable). Ernest Renan's equally celebrated *Vie de Jesus* ("Life of Jesus"; 1863) represents the highpoint of the liberal "lives," offering the world the pale and timeless Galilean whom the next generation would reject as too ephemeral, almost too effeminate, for the needs of a brave new age.

It was Schweitzer himself, of course, who rejected the liberal portraits most sharply and effectively. For Schweitzer, Reimarus was right to see Jesus in the context of first-century Judaism, but wrong to see him as a revolutionary. Instead, the first-century phenomenon which Jesus shared with his contemporaries was "apocalyptic," the expectation of the imminent end of the world. Schweitzer's brilliant exposition and critique of the work of others is matched only by the daring and boldness of his own silhouette of Jesus. We cannot know him except by obeying his summons; he is the totally different Jesus, the Jesus unlike all our expectations. He believed himself to be the Messiah while the onlookers thought he might be Elijah; he confidently expected that his God would step in and bring the world to an end during the course of his ministry. He dreamed the impossible dream of the kingdom, bringing about the end of world history. When this did not happen, and the great wheel of history refused to turn, he threw himself upon it, was crushed in the process, but succeeded in turning it nonetheless. He thus took upon himself the Great Affliction, which was to break upon Israel and the world. The bridge between his historical life and Christianity is formed by his *personality:* he towers over history, and calls people to follow him in changing the world. The very failure of his hopes sets them free from Jewish shackles, to become, in their new guise, the hope of the world. The main lines of Schweitzer's silhouette remain stark and striking nearly a century later.

In a measure, Schweitzer succeeded. Almost all western thought about Jesus has taken his basic ideas on board in some way or another. In their very strangeness they carried, perhaps, more conviction than they should have done. People's attention was arrested, and they thought to see Jesus, because Schweitzer had the skill to make them see darkening apocalyptic skies, secrets being hidden and revealed, the strange shadows of a coming cataclysm, and the silhouette of a cross upon a hill, and to hear with him, in the strange summons to the disciples, the eternal vocation to obedience, conflict, suffering and, finally, knowledge. Those who have drawn back from the full implications of Schweitzer's Jesus have done so, perhaps, just as much because of the total demand such a Jesus makes as because the work failed to meet the exacting standards of historical scholarship. Many other works that have become far more popular fare no better by that criterion. The race is not always to the swift.

My own hypothesis stands in an ambiguous relation to the Old Quest—hardly surprising, considering the ambiguities inherent in that movement itself. On the one hand, the nineteenth-century writers were, in the main, attempting to meet the critical challenge by writing lives of Jesus that seemed to have some historical grounding and yet maintained a semblance of theological, or at least religious, significance. I too wish to write history without forgetting the possible "meaning" the events may possess (Wright 1992a:109–18). On the other hand, nineteenth-century historians frequently ignored the Jewishness of Jesus, trying as hard as they could to universalize him, to make him the timeless teacher of eternal verities. This strand of their work, which served the interests of the romantic-idealist interpretation of Jesus, means that very few of their historical judgments can now stand unaltered. I share their desire to do both history and theology; but their governing hermeneutical program and consequent historical method mean that I cannot in the end proceed in the same direction as they did.

Schweitzer himself recognized very clearly that, at the turn of the century, the scholar researching Jesus was faced with quite a stark choice. His label for this forms the title of his last main chapter: "Thoroughgoing Scepticism and Thoroughgoing Eschatology." Or, to put it personally, the choice between the view of William Wrede and that of Schweitzer himself. Since this antithesis, in one form or another, still faces us at the end of the twentieth century, it is worth sketching it out a little more.

Wrede and Schweitzer both, in their own way, offered a development of Reimarus' basic position. Both thought that serious historical study of Jesus would come up with something very different to what mainstream orthodoxy had supposed or wanted (Schweitzer 1954:329–30). But there the ways divided. Wrede's book on the "Messianic secret" in Mark went further than Reimarus: all we know of Jesus is that he was a Galilean teacher or prophet who did and said some striking things and was eventually executed (ibid:336). Mark's Gospel, from which the others derive, is a theologically motivated fiction, devised from within an early church that had already substantially altered direction away from Jesus' own agenda. Schweitzer, however, while agreeing with Reimarus that Jesus belongs within his first-century Jewish context, insisted that the Jewish context that mattered was not revolution, but apocalyptic. On this basis he was able to include within his own sketch far more gospel material than Wrede, and to suggest a far more nuanced development from Jesus, through the early church, to the writing of the Gospels.

Once the distinction between these two positions is fully grasped, we can understand the two main highways of critical writing about Jesus in the late twentieth century. The *Wredestrasse* insists that we know comparatively little about Jesus, and that the Gospels, in outline and detail, contain a great deal that reflects only the concerns of the early church. The *Schweitzerstrasse* places Jesus within the context of apocalyptic Judaism, and on that basis postulates far more continuity between Jesus himself, the early church, and the Gospels, while allowing of course for importantly different historical settings in each case. The two approaches are sufficiently distinct for us to be able to categorize current writings in two main groups (discussed in Wright 1996:28–124). Of course, these days the *Strasse* has in each case turned into an *Autobahn,* with a lot of people going, at different speeds, in a lot of different lanes and indeed directions. This development, in turn, has spawned a good many side-roads, service-stations and picnic-areas. Several writers, also, have tried to erect new link-roads and junctions between the two main routes. But the distinction between them remains illuminating, as we shall see in due course. Do we know rather little about Jesus, with the Gospels offering us a largely misleading portrait (Wrede)? Or was Jesus an apocalyptic Jewish prophet, with the Gospels reflecting, within their own contexts, a good deal about his proclamation of the kingdom (Schweitzer)?

No Quest to New Quest: Schweitzer to Schillebeeckx

Albert Schweitzer is thus the turning-point in the history of the "Quest." He demolished the old "Quest" so successfully—and provided such a shocking alternative—that for half a century serious scholarship had great difficulty in working its way back to history when dealing with Jesus. This was the period of the great *via negativa,* when theologians applied to Jesus that tradition of reverent silence which in other traditions had been reserved for speaking about the one God. Martin Kähler had already issued his protest in this direction in 1892: the preached Christ should be the focal point of theology, and if Jesus and hence the true God are to be known only through history, then the historians will become the priests. (Instead, Kähler seems to leave the preacher in control.) In 1926 Bultmann published *Jesus and the Word* (ET 1958), in which he discarded the apocalyptic trappings of the preaching of Jesus, and the "wishful thinking about the world to come," and translated the eschatology of Jesus into the existentialist call for decision. Like Schweitzer, he rejected the nineteenth-century liberal Protestant Jesus; unlike Schweitzer, he insisted that Jesus' "personality" could not be recovered from the records, and would in any case have been of no interest for theology. The stories which looked like stories of the historical Jesus were mostly faith-statements about the "risen Christ" read back into his lifetime, expressing therefore the current faith of the church rather than historical memory. In any case, Jesus shared the primitive and mythological outlook of his day, and one would have to get back behind that (by "demythologization") if one wished to uncover the "real" import of his message. The bridge between Jesus and the life of the church was then to be found simply in the preaching of the Word (Bultmann 1958:218–19). Bultmann trod the fine line between having no interest in the historical Jesus and wanting to keep him on his own side just in case. Separated from both his Jewish context and the post-Easter church (a separation reinforced by the "criterion of dissimilarity"), such a Jesus is almost as lonely a figure as Schweitzer's, though for a different reason.

Bultmann in his way, and Karl Barth in his, ensured that little was done to advance genuine historical work on Jesus in the years between the wars. Attention was focused instead on early Christian faith and experience, in the belief that there, rather than in a dubiously reconstructed Jesus, lay the key to the divine revelation that was presumed to have taken place in early Christianity. Form criticism, the tool usually associated with Bultmann, was not, at its heart, designed to find out about Jesus. It was part of the other great "Quest," which still goes on despite being in principle even harder than the Quest for Jesus: the Quest for the Kerygmatic Church, the attempt to reconstruct movements of thought and belief in the first century, and in particular to recapture (in both senses) the early Christian faith. The Gospels are faith-documents, not history books. The echoes of Melanchthon are not far away: Bultmann intended to direct attention to faith rather than "bare facts"; but the echoes of Reimarus and Wrede are there too, in the distinction between "what really happened" and the beliefs of the church, including those of the Gospel writers. The difference is that Reimarus was directing attention to the history in order to undermine the theology. Bultmann, in effect, rejected the challenge by denying the premises. History had nothing to do with faith.

Books about Jesus, of course, continued to be written. Some of them were, so to speak, nineteenth-century "lives" written a little too late, not really taking Schweitzer's challenge on board. Others, exemplified by a scholar like T. W. Manson, attempted to take the historical questions seriously but without integrating the detailed work into a large picture that would have given direction to further study. In this phase too one might put the work of Joachim Jeremias and C. H. Dodd, neither of whom fit too easily into any of the "movements" so beloved of scholars. But, on the continent, it turned out that a vow of silence was not easy to maintain. Despite all the pressing theological reasons for not wanting to enquire about Jesus, the boldest of Bultmann's pupils realized that this time the master had gone too far.

On 23 October 1953, Ernst Käsemann gave a now-famous lecture to a group of former Bultmann students on "The Problem of the Historical Jesus" (1964:15–47), thereby beginning a significantly new phase, which quickly styled itself "The New Quest for the Historical Jesus." Käsemann,

aware (as in all his work) of the dangers of idealism and docetism, insisted that if Jesus was not
earthed in history then he might be pulled in any
direction, might be made the hero of any theological or political program. Käsemann had in
mind, undoubtedly, the various Nazi theologies
that had been able, in the absence of serious
Jesus-study in pre-war Germany, to construct a
largely un-Jewish Jesus. Without knowing who it
was who died on the cross, he said, there would be
no solid ground for upholding the gospel of the
cross in all its sharpness, which he saw as especially needed in post-war Germany. However, this
very definite theological agenda, for all its worth
(which would scarcely be questioned today),
meant that the New Quest, ironically enough, did
not represent a turning to history in the fullest
sense. The best known of the books to appear during this phase, that of Günther Bornkamm, begins
with words already quoted: "No one is any longer
in the position to write a life of Jesus" (1960:1).

The main productions of the New Quest are, in
fact, of little lasting value. Its practitioners, or
would-be practitioners, have not shaken off the
outdated view of apocalyptic as meaning simply
the expectation of the end of the world, in a
crudely literalistic sense. Nor have they managed
to escape from the constraining shackles of form-
and tradition-criticism, which, being mainly
designed to discover the early church, not Jesus
himself, have caused considerable difficulty when
it comes to serious historical reconstruction. For
this reason, much time has been devoted to
method, and in particular to discussing the appropriate criteria for reconstructing the life of Jesus—

a concern which leads, with a sad inevitability, to books filled with footnotes, in which the trees are so difficult to discern that one never even glimpses the forest itself (see, for example, the four methodological surveys in Epp and McRae 1989:75–198). Attention has been focused on sayings of Jesus, both within and outside the synoptic tradition. This, again, is true to the Reformation emphasis: the purpose of Jesus' life was to *say* things, to teach great truths in a timeless fashion. It was also true to idealist philosophy: what matters ultimately is ideas, not events.

One of the largest works from this period—that is, between Schweitzer and the Third Quest, which has arisen in the last fifteen years—is that of the Dominican theologian Edward Schillebeeckx. His prodigious book on Jesus builds on the traditio-historical criticism whereby the Synoptic Gospels have been combed for evidence of this or that "early Christian community," and between whose faith-statements glimpses of Jesus may emerge. Such an argument is necessarily both tortuous and tenuous, since different sets of traditio-historical critics will come out with different sets of answers. Schillebeeckx takes a position that is the mirror-image of Bultmann's: the resurrection accounts are stories from Jesus' lifetime, brought forwards. His eventual leap from a purely historical Jesus to the incarnate Son of God is based on little or nothing in the main part of the book itself. He seems to lend considerable tacit support to the notion that history and theology are two worlds that must be kept entirely separate. His book bravely attempts to combine the multiple hypotheses required to postulate both a divided

"Q community," as a key matrix of early traditions, and some sort of normative theological interest. But his work seems to me to have shown the barrenness of the New Quest in just as devastating (though not as readable) a way as Schweitzer's did in relation to the Old.

Not that the New Quest is finished. (Perhaps I should state at this point that I do not actually believe in rigid "periods" in the history of scholarship, except as heuristic aids to help us grasp currents of thought. In the present matter, it would be silly to imagine that all scholars suddenly gave up one kind of work and took up another—just as silly, in fact, as the impression given by many surveys of Gospel scholarship in this century, in which suddenly "everyone" is doing form criticism, redaction criticism, or whatever.) Followers of the Wrede-Bultmann line are numerous, and, after a comparatively quiet period in the 1980s, they are again back in business. They have not given up trying out the combinations and permutations of the master's arguments, endlessly discussing criteria, reconstructing Q, and, most recently, setting up a new Seminar. This work has now produced quite substantial results, and in the next chapter we must look at them. First, however, a summary of where we have got to so far.

Two Hundred Years of Questing

What did the Quest achieve in the two hundred years between Reimarus and Schillebeeckx? It put the historical question firmly and irrevocably on the theological map, but without providing a definite answer to it. Theologians cannot honestly ignore the questions of who Jesus was, whether he said and did roughly what we find in the Gospels, the reasons for his death, and the reasons for the rise of Christianity. This is by no means to imply that the historical study of Jesus is designed simply for the benefit of the church and theology. Those who wish to demonstrate the unbelievability of Christianity, as did Reimarus and some of his followers, are likewise bound to take these questions seriously. But have the historians enabled either side, or indeed those in the middle, to get very far?

Looking simply, for now, at the period between Schweitzer and Schillebeeckx, we find many notable works in the field of systematic theology, and particularly Christology. All of them have made use, to a lesser or greater extent, of the figure of Jesus. The massive schemes of writers like Karl Barth and Paul Tillich, the provocative and seminal works of Wolfhart Pannenberg, Eberhard Jüngel, and Jürgen Moltmann, and the great Catholic works of Karl Rahner, Walter Kasper, Piet Schoonenberg, and Edward Schillebeeckx himself—not to mention Hans Küng's famous *On Being a Christian*—all bear witness to the importance of the question of the historical Jesus within their respective schemes (for details, see McGrath 1994). But at no point, I suggest, has the full impact of the historical evidence been allowed to influence very much the dogmatic conclusions reached; when it has, it is only perhaps as a concession. This may seem an over-hasty judgment: some of these theologians (one thinks particularly of Pannenberg) have made very serious and thorough use of parts of Jesus' Jewish context; but I remain convinced that there is a good deal more to be said about the perceptions, worldviews, and mindsets of first-century Jews that will have considerable importance, as yet unimagined, for systematic theology. The exception to this might be the liberation theologians, among whom Segundo in particular has produced an impressive study (1985). But there again the conclusions, though very different from the normal dogmatic ones, seem to have been at least outlined in advance; the detailed historical work has not really been taken with full seriousness.

The years of the silhouette were by no means all negative. Even if they did not reach firm results about Jesus, they provided new pictures of the early church. These turn out to be the twentieth-century equivalent of the nineteenth-century lives of Jesus (see Wright 1992a:341–58): fanciful, theory-laden, and agenda-driven hypotheses about the early church, with only tangential relation to the sources, and to the actual history of first-century Palestine, Asia Minor, and elsewhere. But, again like their nineteenth-century analogue, they bear witness both to the complexity of the task, to its potential theological importance, and, negatively, to the wrongness of many theories which, having now been tried and found wanting, ought to be consigned to the scrap-heap. Out of all this there might perhaps grow a new awareness of the first-century history and its potential theological significance.

Two hundred years, then—surveyed swiftly here, because the story has been told so often—have demonstrated that the Quest is vital, but difficult. The sources are no less tricky to use now than they were at the start. The questions are no less pressing. From time to time one hopes that a few false trails may have been closed off for good, but, just when one allows oneself a sigh of relief at the thought, there arises another cunning variation on an old theme (Wright 1992a:339–476). From time to time one believes that some aspect of first-century Jewish history is now firmly established, so that it can be used as a fixed point in future work; but there always seems to be enough scope within the complex sources for strikingly different interpretations to emerge. Nevertheless, the last twenty years (1975 to 1995) have seen a remarkable flurry of research, addressing all these questions with renewed vigor and enthusiasm.

2
The New Quest Renewed?

Albert Schweitzer bequeathed two stark alternatives to posterity: the "thoroughgoing skepticism"
of William Wrede, and his own "thoroughgoing
eschatology." As we turn to the current scene in
Jesus-studies, we discover that these two streets
have become broad highways with a good deal of
traffic all trying to use them at once. In the present chapter we shall consider those who, in some
senses at least, have followed Wrede; in the following chapter, those who have followed
Schweitzer.

The Jesus Seminar

The late 1970s and early 1980s saw a decline in the
New Quest, and, as we shall see presently, the rise
of a quite different approach. But in the mid-1980s
a serious move was made to put new life into what
remains basically the post-Bultmannian study of
Jesus. In 1985 Robert W. Funk, then Professor in
the University of Montana, founded the Jesus
Seminar, bringing together scholars in North

America to discuss sayings of Jesus piece by piece and to vote on their authenticity or otherwise.

The agenda and practice of this Seminar contained three important features. First, all relevant Jesus-material was to be included. The net was cast far wider than the canonical Gospels, bringing in *Thomas* and numerous other works, several of them fragmentary. Second, voting took place in four categories, using colored beads that symbolize different grades of probability: red meant authentic, pink probably authentic, gray probably inauthentic, black definitely inauthentic. And third, the Seminar published its results as widely as possible, recognizing that it is not only scholars who might be interested in the results.

There are two points in particular, however, at which criticism must be leveled. The underlying presuppositions of the enterprise were systematically unclear, and the way the system actually operated gave cause for concern. In the Introduction to the red-letter text of Mark we were told that scholars were united on the major premises that underlie all critical work on the Gospels. Unfortunately, the whole point of a premise is that it is not a conclusion, whereas most of the statements offered as premises in what follows are conclusions, many of them very dubious.

The Seminar's actual practice of assigning "weighted averages" to the different votes cast was also an issue. Obviously, if 25 percent of Fellows voted in each category, there would have been a stalemate, and no coloring would have been possible; so some system for deciding how to proceed was necessary. But in several instances a high percentage—sometimes a clear majority—voted either red or pink, i.e. either authentic or probably authentic, but the weighted average came out gray because of the high proportion of black votes cast on the other side. A voting system like this, allied to a publicity machine that purported to tell America "what Jesus really said," had nothing whatever to commend it.

John Dominic Crossan

Crossan's major work, *The Historical Jesus: The Life of a Mediterranean Jewish Peasant,* is a book to treasure for its learning, its thoroughness, its brilliant handling of multiple and complex issues, its amazing inventiveness, and above all, its sheer readability. It is all the more frustrating, therefore, to have to conclude that the book is almost entirely wrong.

Crossan follows Wrede in believing that Mark (and following him, Matthew and Luke) has bequeathed to subsequent history an account of Jesus that, though beguilingly attractive, is fundamentally fictitious. Mark, like a brilliant scriptwriter, shows us a story-line so compelling that he lures us into imagining that it is really historical.

Crossan follows Bultmann in certain key respects that justify our placing of him within the revived Bultmannian New Quest. True, he actually thinks (against Bultmann) that we can know a good deal about Jesus, and that what we can know is significant for Christian faith and practice. By implication at least, Crossan's Jesus sets standards against which subsequent developments in the tradition can be judged (Crossan

1991:263). Crossan also thinks, against Bultmann, that history must be read politically rather than existentially, and that the Bultmannian hermeneutic never engages (as he wants to do) with systemic evil, but only with personal evil. He studies not only Jesus' words, but also his deeds; indeed, the words themselves are "performance," so that the very opening sentence of Crossan's largest work, in which this is highlighted, is intended to distance himself from Bultmann (1991:xi).

Crossan argues that Jesus was trying to inaugurate "the brokerless kingdom of God." Jesus was encouraging all and sundry, but especially the "nobodies," to rely on God alone, subverting the whole patron/client system. He was not setting himself up as a new sort of "patron"; that was why he kept on the move, lest any one town or village would regard him as such and set itself up as his intermediaries in a renewed patronage system, brokering his religious authority (1991: 346ff., 422).

The heart of Jesus' activity is seen in the highly subversive combination of "magic and meal." Magic is a miracle done by the wrong person; and commensality, the sharing of food, was equally powerful as a socially and spiritually subversive action. "The heart of the original Jesus movement" was "a shared egalitarianism of spiritual and material resources" (1991:341). As a result, Jesus is to be seen as a *peasant Jewish Cynic*, like and unlike other Cynics of the period.

What can be said about this remarkable vision of Jesus and his work? Certainly not that it illegitimately turns Jesus' concern in a social direction. I am convinced that the social and material dimensions of Jesus' ministry must be brought to the fore, as indeed they are in many contemporary writings. My anxiety, rather, is this: in grasping the way in which Jesus' program cut against the normal social expectations of Mediterranean peasant culture, Crossan has radically and consistently underplayed the specifically Jewish dimension both of the culture itself and of Jesus' agenda for it.

Crossan's rejection of apocalyptic, as incommensurate with Jesus' agenda, shows through in his dismissal of the Jewish hope which, in my reading (and that of several others), Jesus claimed to fulfill. His reconstruction enables us to understand perfectly well why there would be opposition to Jesus. But he never explains why there would be hostility from Jews as Jews, from those who saw themselves as guardians of Israel's beliefs, hopes, and way of life. In Crossan's view, the earliest followers of Jesus knew nothing whatever about the details of why or how Jesus died, except that he had been crucified. With his reconstruction of the genesis of the passion narratives, we are back again in the realm of William Wrede. Once you doubt everything in the story, and postulate a chain of events by which someone might have taken it upon themselves to invent such a narrative from scratch, all things are possible. But not all things are probable.

I began this analysis of Crossan's work by saying that he is one of the most brilliant New Testament scholars alive today. Sharp disagreement should not make the praise sound faint. Crossan has attempted to reconstruct the whole of early Christianity, with massive labor and attention to detail; with scintillating hypotheses right, left, and center; with a sense of the big picture as well as the little detail; with an eye open for contemporary implications of his historical work; and, perhaps most of all, with a deft, shrewd, and impish writing style that make us smile with appreciation at the very moment when we most want to disagree. We may say of Crossan, as he says of Mark, that he is such a gifted scriptwriter that we are lured into imagining that his scheme is actually historical.

Like Odysseus, however, we must resist the siren's voice. Crossan towers above the rest of the renewed "New Quest" in just the same way as Schweitzer and Bultmann tower above most of twentieth-century scholarship, and for much the same reasons. He, like them, has had the courage to see the whole picture, to think his hypothesis through to the end, to try out radically new ideas, to write it all up in a highly engaging manner, and to debate it publicly without acrimony. With foes like this, who needs friends? May the debate continue.

3
Back to the Future:
The "Third Quest"

Breaking Out of the Straitjacket

The "New Quest" was the first sign that the wall of resistance to serious study of Jesus had begun to crack. Now the dam has burst altogether, allowing a flood of scholarly and seriously historical books on Jesus to sweep the market in the space of a very few years. Instead of the Old Quest brought to a close by Albert Schweitzer, and the New Quest inaugurated by Ernst Käsemann (and revived by the Jesus Seminar), we now have a phenomenon which is arguably sufficiently distinct to deserve the title of a "Third Quest" (Neill and Wright 1988:379–403). There are some writers who straddle the revived "New Quest" and the "Third Quest." Instances would include Geza Vermes (who stresses the Jewishness of Jesus, but ends up with an existentialist teacher), and Marcus Borg (who puts Jesus firmly in his Jewish social and cultural context, but ends up with Jesus as a non-apocalyptic sage, teacher, prophet, and movement-founder). There are considerable affinities, too, between Crossan and Richard Horsley, such as to make the placing of them in different categories dubious. Let me stress again that, though there are vital distinctions to be drawn, the categories are heuristic attempts to describe recent writing, not watertight compartments. However, I have come to the view that the distinction which Schweitzer drew between himself and Wrede still has a lot to commend it; that those who follow Schweitzer in placing Jesus within apocalyptic Jewish eschatology belong in a category distinct from those who do not; and that this category is where the real leading edge of contemporary Jesus-scholarship is to be found.

There are, up to the mid-1990s, twenty writers that I regard as particularly important within this Third Quest. In chronological order of publication in English, they are Caird (1965), Brandon (1967), Betz (1968 [1965]), Hengel (1971, 1973, 1981b [1968]), Vermes (1973, 1983, 1993), Meyer (1979, 1992a, 1992b), Chilton (1979, 1984, 1992), Riches (1980), Harvey (1982, 1990), Lohfink (1984), Borg (1984, 1987a, 1994b), Sanders (1985, 1993), Oakman (1986), Theissen (1987), Horsley (1987), Freyne (1988), Charlesworth (1988), Witherington (1990, 1994, 1995), Meier (1991, 1994), and de Jonge (1991a). Charlesworth gives a useful annotated list (187-207) of writing on Jesus in the 1980s. See also, in various slightly different categories: Dodd 1971; Yoder 1994 [1972]; Bowker 1973; Derrett 1973; Maccoby 1980 [1973]; Dunn 1975; O'Neill 1980, 1995; Farmer 1982 (building on Farmer 1956, a work which could have precip-

itated the Third Quest earlier if more notice had
been taken of it); Schüssler Fiorenza 1983, 1994;
Bammel & Moule 1984; Rivkin 1984; Buchanan
1984; Riesner 1984 [1981]; Goergen 1986a,
1986b; Leivestad 1987; Zeitlin 1988; Stanton
1989; Neusner 1993; Brown 1994; Johnson 1995
(though this work denies the propriety of any
"quest" at all, it nevertheless makes oblique con-
tributions to it); O'Collins 1995. Mention should
also be made of the Hensley Henson lectures of
Professor Colin Brown, delivered in Oxford in
1993, building on his previous work in various
places (e.g., Brown 1984). Anyone familiar with
these books will at once see how very different
many of them are from each other, and yet how
similar are the sets of questions being addressed—
which are the questions that I believe really need
discussing.

I have already discussed several of these works
elsewhere. The reader may be glad to know that
there is nothing to be gained by repeating myself
at this point, or by attempting to go through the
list, author by author, offering exposition and critique (see Neill and Wright 1988:379–403; Wright
1992b). A better method of reviewing the Third
Quest, as a prelude to my own exposition, will be
to examine the questions that all these writers are
addressing, drawing out their particular emphases
as we do so. More detail, and more debate, is
available in Wright 1996.

First, though, some general remarks about the
Third Quest. There is now a real attempt to do history seriously. Josephus, so long inexplicably
ignored, is suddenly and happily in vogue. There

is a real willingness to be guided by first-century sources, and to see the Judaism of that period in all its complex pluriformity, with the help now available from modern studies of the history and literature of the period (Wright 1992:339–464). Qumran and the apocalyptic writings are not merely part of the dark backcloth against which the great light of the gospel shines the more brightly; they are part of the historical evidence for the world of first-century Palestine. Certain basic questions emerge: Jesus' message is evaluated, not for its timeless significance, but for the meaning it must have had for the audience of his own day, who had their minds full of poverty and politics, and would have had little time for theological abstractions or timeless verities. The crucifixion, long recognized as an absolute bedrock in history, is now regularly made the center of understanding: what must Jesus have been like if he ended up on a Roman cross? The answer given by S. G. F. Brandon (himself one recent representative in a long line) is now usually rejected: Jesus was not the would-be instigator of a violent Jewish uprising (Bammel and Moule 1984). But Brandon's mistake was not as silly as some have supposed. It cannot be dismissed by means of the old division of politics and theology, reflecting the expensive luxury of post-Enlightenment dualism. The question still presses, as to whether Jesus in any way sided with those who wanted to overthrow Rome.

If we start out with historical questions such as these, there are important consequences for our method. We do not need to detach Jesus' sayings from the rest of the evidence, and examine them in isolation. The words of Jesus in the gospel tradition have been studied endlessly without hearing the *ipsissima vox Jesu* ("the actual voice of Jesus") any the clearer, and without resolving the enigma of the christological titles. This is the burden of Sanders' section on method, and I think he is right (Sanders 1985:3–13, 133). The Old Quest was determined that Jesus should look as little like a first-century Jew as possible. Bultmann was determined that, though Jesus was historically a first-century Jew, his first-century Jewishness was precisely not the place where his "significance" lay. The renewed "New Quest," following this line, has often played down the specifically Jewish features of Jesus, stressing instead those which he may have shared with other Mediterranean cultures; it has also downplayed to a large extent the significance of Jesus' death, stressing that we know very little about it and suggesting that the earliest Christians were not particularly interested in it—a feature, of course, which marks a break with Bultmann himself. The present "Third Quest," by and large, will have none of this. Jesus must be understood as a comprehensible and yet, so to speak, crucifiable first-century Jew, whatever the theological or hermeneutical consequences.

To this extent, the old so-called "criterion of dissimilarity" may still be applied, though with great caution. Plenty of Jews were not, in this sense, crucifiable; plenty of early Christians were less comprehensibly Jewish. There were, of course, thousands of other Jews crucified in Palestine in the same period, but few if any were handed over by Jewish authorities, as Jesus seems to have been. There were many "Jewish Christians" in the first generation of the movement; to begin with, of course, all Christians were Jewish. But their allegiance to Jesus made them, from very early on, far less comprehensible as mainstream Jews (Alexander 1992). This way of setting up a "criterion of dissimilarity" is substantially different from the way in which something by that name has been used in the past, i.e., to distance Jesus from Judaism and from the early church. Instead, it locates him firmly within Judaism, though looking at the reasons why he, and then his followers, were rejected by the Jewish authorities. Likewise, it assumes a major continuity between him and his followers, while respecting the fact that, unlike him, they were from very early on not perceived as simply one more movement within Judaism. This revived "criterion of dissimilarity" cannot be simply applied, as used to be attempted, to saying after saying with any hope of "validating" individual words or sentences. Historians do not live by sayings alone. Instead, the criterion works on a larger scale altogether, to check the lines of a fully historical portrait, including actions and words within the wider treatment of Jesus' aims. This, as we saw in the first volume, is what serious history is all about (Wright 1992a:81–120).

In writing and rewriting *Jesus and the Victory of God* (1996), I sometimes wished that the substance of this present argument—and indeed of *The New Testament and the People of God* chapter 4 (Wright 1992a:81–120)—could be included in the running head for every page on which synoptic material is under discussion. Perhaps all one can do at this stage is to quote Bultmann and Sanders:

"One can go on asking questions like this about one saying after another, without getting any further" (Bultmann 1968:105); the conviction "that a sufficiently careful exegesis of the sayings material will lead to 'a correct decision' has led many a New Testament scholar into a quagmire from which he has never emerged" (Sanders 1985:131). If someone replies that we should therefore be content never to know anything, perhaps the best answer is that of Charlesworth, who tells of how he abandoned his previous admiration for New Testament scholars who were "cautiously reticent until they [could] defend virtually infallible positions." It is, he says, "wise and prudent to be cautious; but, pushed to extremes, even a virtue can become a vice. As the rabbis stated, timidity is not a virtue in pursuing truth" (Charlesworth 1988:17–18).

And the pursuit of truth—historical truth—is what the Third Quest is all about. Serious historical method, as opposed to the pseudo-historical use of homemade "criteria," is making a comeback in the Third Quest. The much-vaunted "normal critical tools," particularly form criticism, are being tacitly (and in my view rightly) bypassed in the search for Jesus; inquiry is proceeding by means of a proper, and often clearly articulated, method of hypothesis and verification (Meyer 1979:87–92; Sanders 1985:10, 18–22). As we saw in the first volume, and again in the previous chapters, much of the impetus for form-critical and redaction-critical study came from the presupposition that this or that piece of synoptic material about Jesus *could not* be historical; in other words, that *an historical hypothesis about Jesus could already be presupposed* which demanded a further tradition-historical hypothesis to explain the evidence. If, however, a viable alternative historical hypothesis, whether about Jesus or about the early church, is proposed, argued out, and maintained, the need for tradition-criticism within the search for Jesus (to say nothing about its undoubted value in other historical enterprises) could in principle be substantially reduced and altered in shape. This is exactly what happens in the hypotheses of (say) Sanders and Meyer: all sorts of things in the Gospels which, on the Bultmannian paradigm, needed to be explained by complex epicycles of *Traditionsgeschichte* (tradition history) turn out, after all, to fit comfortably within the ministry of Jesus.

It is vital that this point of method be grasped from the outset. Within the Third Quest, which is where I locate *Jesus and the Victory of God,* the task before the serious historian of Jesus is not in the first instance conceived as the reconstruction of traditions about Jesus, according to their place within the history of the early church, but the advancement of serious historical hypotheses— that is, the telling of large-scale narratives—about Jesus himself, and the examination of the *prima facie* relevant data to see how they fit. I am only too aware of how controversial this will seem in certain quarters (also, of how obvious and commonsensical it will seem in others). I am, however, optimistic that the point is being grasped within the Third Quest, which is by no means a narrowly confined movement, since it encompasses scholars of widely differing background and outlook. I am, after all, suggesting no more than that Jesus be studied like any other figure of the ancient past. Nobody grumbles at a book on Alexander the Great if, in telling the story, the author "harmonizes" two or three sources; that is his or her job, to advance hypotheses which draw together the data into a coherent framework rather than leaving it scattered. Of course, sources on Alexander, like sources on Jesus, Tiberius, Beethoven, Gandhi, or anybody else, have their own point of view, which must be taken carefully into account. But the object of the exercise is to produce a coherent synthesis which functions as a hypothesis and must be treated as such (Moule 1984; Wright 1992a:113–15). As I tried to show in *The New Testament and the People of God* (1992), the problem has been that so-called "radical" criticism has not been radical enough, but has remained largely content with the hypothesis about Jesus (and the early church) that were advanced by Schweitzer and Bultmann, making only minor modifications to them. If we are to create new hypotheses we cannot assume any fixed points taken from the history of scholarship. All must be questioned. This is why it is irrelevant and inappropriate to discuss, at every point in the historical argument, those views that arise from quite different paradigms. Of course Third Quest writers—myself included—are interested in what people from different movements of scholarship made, or make, of this or that parable, aphorism or whatever. The detailed work of the renewed "New Quest," and Crossan in particular, must be kept in mind throughout. But the essential argument must take place at a different level.

If today there is a new wave of historical seriousness about Jesus, there is also a new sense,

well beyond what early redaction-criticism envisaged, that the Gospels are to be seen as texts,
works of literary art, in their own right. This has
sometimes misled scholars into supposing that
they are therefore of less historical value. However, there are signs that a more mature approach is
beginning to emerge. It is becoming apparent that
the authors of at least the Synoptic Gospels,
which still provide the bulk of the relevant source
material, intended to write about Jesus, not just
about their own churches and theology, and that
they substantially succeeded in this intention.

The attempt to set Jesus credibly within his
historical context, then, is once again widely
regarded as a reputable scholarly task. Within
this, the Third Quest can claim certain solid
advantages. First, it takes the total Jewish background extremely seriously. Second, its practitioners have no united theological or political
agenda, unlike the quite monochrome New Quest
and its fairly monochrome renewal; the diverse
backgrounds of the scholars involved serve to
provide checks and balances, so that one scholar's reading of a particular passage (say) in Josephus is balanced by another's, and a measure of
critical realism is both possible and increasingly
actual. Third, there has increasingly been a sense
of homing in on the key questions that have to
be asked if we are to make progress. All these
things have enabled the study of Jesus to rejoin
the mainland of historical work after drifting, for
more years than was good for it, around the
archipelago of theologically motivated methods
and criteria.

The Questions

What, then, are the key questions that have emerged, and how are they being handled within the Third Quest? There are, I suggest, five major questions, with a sixth always waiting in the wings. It is important to realize that these questions are not independent or isolated, but overlap and interlock at various points. Indeed, the interaction between them is one of the most complex and interesting features of the whole discussion. These questions are all raised explicitly within the Third Quest; in fact, no work on Jesus can get off the ground without a position being taken, at least by implication, in relation to them all, though many earlier writers simply presupposed particular answers and carried on from there. However, within the Third Quest itself, different writers have focused on different sets of these questions, and no single writer has given them all, and their integration, equal prominence, as I hope eventually to do (though this lies beyond the scope of the present volume).

The five questions are all subdivisions of the larger question which, I submit, all historians of the first century, no matter what their background, are bound to ask, namely: how do we account for the fact that, by 110 C.E., there was a large and vigorous international movement, already showing considerable diversity, whose founding myth (in a quite "neutral" sense) was a story about one Jesus of Nazareth, a figure of the recent past? How do we get, in other words, from the pluriform Judaism that existed within the

Greco-Roman world of 10 B.C.E. to the pluriform
Judaism and Christianity of 110 C.E.—from (roughly) Herod the Great to Ignatius of Antioch? In
every generation there are one or two scholars
who think this can be done without reference to
Jesus. There are also a few dozen who try to do
it with only minimal reference to him. In both
cases the weight of counter-probability is enormous. Radical innovation has to be ascribed elsewhere, and the only strength of such suggestions
is that, since they build on no evidence at all,
they are hard to attack. This forces us, simply as
historians, to ask: who then was Jesus, what was
he trying to do, what happened to him, and
why? And, just as we can ask such questions
about Paul, or the emperor Claudius, or Tiberius'
hatchet-man Sejanus (all figures of the first century about whom we have a certain amount of
historical evidence), there is every reason to ask
them about Jesus as well. So, sharpening up
these issues into our five main questions: How
does Jesus fit into the Judaism of his day? What
were his aims? Why did he die? How did the
early church come into being, and why did it
take the shape it did? And why are the Gospels
what they are? (It will readily be apparent that
my list of questions is close to that of Sanders
1985:1. However, as we proceed it will also be
clear that he and I understand several of the
questions in interestingly different ways. Sanders
claims to have a non-theological agenda [1985:
333–34; though see Charlesworth 1988:26–29].
He is at least right in this respect, that he is not
attempting to provide a Christian apologetic.)
The sixth question is something of a joker in the

pack, though every writer on Jesus is quite well aware of it: So What?

These questions are emphatically not the mere private concern of Christians and/or theologians. They belong—all of them, including the sixth—in the public arena. They are not "slanted" towards a particular theology, as is clear from the very different answers they receive within the Third Quest itself. To this diversity we now turn.

How Does Jesus Fit into Judaism?

The first question (together with the second, which sharpens it to a point) arises naturally from the whole movement of historical investigation of Jesus. If he belongs anywhere in history, it is within the history of first-century Judaism. But how does he belong there? Was he a typical Jew, really quite unremarkable? Or, at the opposite extreme, was he so totally different that he stood out completely, following an entirely different set of aims, obedient to a different vision of reality? Or, if we renounce these two extremes, did he share the perspective of his people to a large extent, adjusting it only at a few points (however significant) here and there? Or did he have a major program for reform? Where did he fit vis-à-vis the various revolutionary groups, or the Pharisaic movement? Was he a Hasid? A prophet? Did he in any way either encourage or tolerate armed resistance to Rome, or did he speak out against it, or did he ignore the issue? Did he appear in any sense as a Messiah-figure? Where, in short, do we place Jesus within first-century Judaism?

The list of possible answers is of course enormous. To make some sense of them, we may divide

them into three, each of which is capable of considerable variation. The first two can be seen side
by side before we turn to the third.

First, we can put Jesus so thoroughly within his
context as almost to camouflage him into invisi-
bility. Thus we have Jesus the thoroughly Jewish
wandering Hasid (Vermes) and Jesus the Jewish
revolutionary (Brandon). Second, we can put him
at the other extreme, and minimize his Jewishness
(thus moving beyond the boundaries of the Third
Quest). Thus we have Jesus the preacher of timeless
(and non-Jewish) truths (Bultmann), or Jesus the
Cynic (Downing, Mack, and much of the Jesus
Seminar). There are some interesting ways in which
the opposite ends of this chain can be twisted
round so as to meet. Vermes' Jesus, for all he is
supposed to be so very Jewish, preaches in fact a
liberal and timeless form of Judaism which is itself
fairly thoroughly existentialist (Vermes 1993:137).
Crossan's Jesus, for all he is fairly non-Jewish (his
message of the kingdom has little to do with
classic Jewish expectation), preaches a message
opposed to Roman domination, and thus aligns
himself, almost by accident, with some very Jewish movements.

These two extreme positions can of course be
modified. Perhaps, on the one hand, Jesus was
really hoping for violent revolution, but rested
content, for the moment, with secretly gathering
support, waiting for the day when force could and
should be used (Buchanan). Perhaps he was
aligned with a non-violent social revolution, rooted in the peasant society of his day, at the same
time implicitly supporting the "social bandits"
who subsequently, when all else had failed, took to

violence to oppose the system that had systematically brutalized them (Horsley). Perhaps, on the other hand, Jesus was indeed a wandering Cynic-style teacher, but addressed his aphorisms and world-shattering parables to a specifically Jewish context which modified the style and content of the Cynic image, though still aiming its basic thrust at the larger Mediterranean world (Crossan).

The historian is thus faced with a bewildering range of options. One well-worn traditional Christian position is to say that the Jewish background is a mass of legalism and formalism, and that Jesus came to teach a different sort of religion, namely, an interior spiritual sort. This is clearly no good (Sanders 1985:23–47, 331–34). If it were true, Jesus would have been simply incomprehensible, a teacher of abstract and interior truths to a people hungry for God to act within history. The people were asking for bread and freedom, not thin air. Nor did he simply come to found the church, giving the Sermon on the Mount as its charter. In the search for alternatives to these distortions, scholars and exegetes have tried ways of closer integration, usually involving Jesus in some form of affirmation of basic Jewish expectations, with minor modifications here and there. We have Jesus the prophet of "restoration eschatology" (Sanders 1985; 1993). We have Jesus the charismatic of charismatics, the great spiritual leader who shared so completely the aspirations of the Pharisees (Rivkin 1980; 1984). In these portraits, and many others like them, Jesus has little or no quarrel with (what is seen as) mainline Judaism, but only with the official Jerusalem aristocracy, who are then seen as the proximate cause of his death.

If the first two forms of solution are the near-identification and the near-dislocation between Jesus and Judaism, the third explores the confrontation between Jesus and Judaism in terms of Jesus' reclamation of a key part of the Jewish heritage itself. One of the clearest exponents of this point of view is Marcus Borg (1984). For him, Jesus claims the high ground of fulfillment of the Jewish scriptures, in particular the prophets, while challenging head-on several aspects of the actual Judaism of his time. The challenge comes, *not* because he has a different, non-Jewish sort of religion, but because first-century Judaism, including Pharisaism, is in his view disobedient to Israel's God and consequently likely to reap disaster. I do not follow Borg's thesis all the way, and indeed, I take a different direction on several vital issues. But this general thrust, of a very Jewish Jesus who was nevertheless opposed to some high-profile features of first-century Judaism, seems to me the most viable one if we are to do justice, not just to the evidence of the synoptic Gospels (they, after all, are easy game for any critic who wants to avoid their implications) but more particularly to the requirements of consistency and clear historical line in our historical reconstruction of Jesus himself.

We have already noted more than once that "Judaism" is as difficult to describe as Jesus himself (Wright 1992a:145–338), so that putting the two together is like climbing from one moving boat into another. The history of research indicates how easy it is to fall into the water. The more specific questions, which bring the first of our main questions into sharper focus, concern especially Jesus' relationship with the Pharisees, and here the

two boats sometimes seem close to capsizing altogether. Some theories try to keep the conflict to a
minimum: according to Sanders, the Pharisees of
Jesus' day were a small, Jerusalem-based group,
and the narratives which portray Jesus in conflict
with them reflect simply the church-versus-syna-
gogue controversies of a later period. (For discussion and critique, see Wright 1992a:181–203;
Sanders seems to have modified his position in his
more recent book on Judaism [1992], and his second one on Jesus [1993].) Rivkin, however, for all
his desire to show that the Roman imperial system
was responsible for Jesus' death, allows that the
"Scribes-Pharisees" (he considers the two groups
identical) would have had difficulty with much
that Jesus said and did, even though his religious
ideals coincided with theirs to a large extent
(Rivkin 1984:44, 96–99; also Neusner 1993). Other
theories allow for considerable conflict. Riches
sees Pharisaic Judaism as offering a wrong, or at
least deficient, view of the true God, with Jesus
"transforming" this view into the right one (particularly important in his treatment is the "transformation" of the vision of a wrathful God into that
of a merciful one [Riches 1980:130–35]). Borg is
equally concerned to maintain the historicity of
Jesus' challenge to basic Jewish symbols and insti-
tutions, the Torah and the Temple being central.
His Jesus therefore comes into quite sharp conflict
with the Pharisees. But this is not because Judaism
is the wrong sort of religion; it is because Israel
has forgotten her vocation.

A further point at which our answer to the first
question depends upon a careful reconstruction of
one aspect of first-century Judaism is the question

of Jesus' relation to the hopes and aspirations of Israel. Neither Sanders nor Borg deals at all with the question of Jesus' Messiahship in its relation to Israel. If, however, it is true that the Temple was bound up in Jewish thought with the true king (Wright 1992a: 224–26, 307–20; 1996:477– 539), then Sanders' argument that Jesus' attitude to the Temple is the best starting-point for the historical quest is *ipso facto* an argument for the centrality of Messiahship within Jesus' self-understanding, or at the very least within his contemporaries' understanding of him. And "Messiahship" in this context is not (as, surprisingly, even Vermes seems to think) a "divine" category. It is an "Israel" category. Jesus as "king of the Jews" is the one in whom Israel's destiny is summed up, as Pilate knew very well when he caused the *titulus* to be nailed to the cross, offering thereby an insult to the nation, as much as to its supposed (and now supposedly failed) Messiah.

Sharpening up still further the question of Jesus and Jewish aspirations, we continually meet the question: did Jesus, or did he not, expect the end of the world, i.e., of the space-time universe? Here the two boats are again in choppy water. Did Jews expect the end of the world? If so, did Jesus share that expectation, or react against it? If not, did he introduce the idea? Some, such as Harvey, follow Schweitzer and Bultmann in saying "yes" in both cases: Jesus, like first-century Jews, did expect the end of the world. Others, such as Mack, say "yes" and "no": many Jews did cherish "apocalyptic" expectations (meaning by that an end-of-the-world expectation), but Jesus took a different line. Others, such as Borg (1984; 1987b), echo the protests of writers like Caird and Glasson, with a double negative: neither Jesus nor his Jewish contemporaries expected the end of the world (Caird 1965; 1980: chaps. 12–14; Glasson 1984). This leaves yet a further question: did he then use apocalyptic imagery in his preaching, and if so how are we to understand it? One can deny the authenticity of the "apocalyptic" sayings, or one can reinterpret them: Perrin does the first (1967:202–6), Borg the second (throughout his writings). Sanders, in his book on Jesus, leaves this issue finely balanced (1985); in his more recent work he seems to me to be coming down more on the side of Borg and others. This whole problem, of course, has a sting in its tail in the form of an implication for the sixth question: if Jesus expected the end of the world, then he was mistaken, so was he perhaps mistaken about all sorts of other things as well? (This last suggestion usually, as a matter of fact, devalues the debate. Anyone who says that Jesus did not expect the end of the world may find themselves suspected of having cooked the evidence to "protect" Jesus' reputation—unless, of course, the conclusion is advanced within the "Jesus Seminar," where it is evidence of a desire for a non-apocalyptic, and hence non-fundamentalist or non-Reaganite, Jesus!) We need here to be sure what exactly we are talking about; we need to be on firm ground in our reading of apocalyptic language and literature. A brief word on both, by way of recapitulation from *The New Testament and the People of God,* is appropriate at this stage.

First, what are we talking about in discussing first-century Jewish hopes? It has commonly been assumed, at least since Weiss and Schweitzer, that

Jesus and many of his contemporaries expected the imminent end of the present space-time order altogether, the winding up of history and the ushering in of a new age in radical discontinuity with the present one. It is possible, however, to take the idea in quite a different sense: that Jesus and some of his contemporaries expected the end of the present *world order,* i.e., the end of the period when the Gentiles were lording it over the people of the true God, and the inauguration of the time when this God would take his power and reign and, in the process, restore the fortunes of his suffering people. Clarity at this point is imperative. One can either opt for extreme discontinuity, or extreme continuity, or find some way (as Sanders tries to do) of holding both together.

Second, how does apocalyptic language and literature work? In the post-Bultmannian New Quest it was assumed that talk of the "kingdom of god," or the "son of man coming on the clouds of heaven," was to be taken as a literal prediction of events, shortly to take place, which would close the space-time order. But not only is it unnecessary to read apocalyptic language in this way: it is actually necessary, as historians, that we refuse to do so. Apocalyptic language was (among many other things, to be sure) an elaborate metaphor-system for investing historical events with theological significance. This understanding of the literature has at any rate a good *prima facie* claim to be historically on target, in contrast with the contrived literalism in which the Bultmann school find themselves as uncomfortable bedfellows of mainstream fundamentalism.

What then was Jesus talking about? It is time (as I argue in detail in 1996:320–68) to reject the old idea that Jesus expected the end of the space-time universe—though this does not mean, as the "Jesus Seminar" has imagined, that Jesus did not use "apocalyptic" language. Nor does it mean, as I find myself accused of saying by some colleagues, that we have hereby "abandoned eschatology." Far from it. I wish to stress that, in my view, first-century Judaism, and Jesus as firmly within it, can be understood only within a climate of intense eschatological expectation, whose character I have already tried to make clear (Wright 1992a:268–338). If this position is taken, it becomes possible to move, as Caird did, to the claim that Jesus' warnings about imminent judgment were intended to be taken as denoting (what we would call) socio-political events, *seen as the climactic moment in Israel's history,* and, in consequence, as constituting a summons to *national* repentance. In this light, Jesus appears as a successor to Jeremiah and his like, warning Israel that persistence in her present course will bring political disaster, which in turn should be *understood as* the judgment of Israel's own God. But Jesus is not merely a successor, one in a continuing line of prophets. His warnings include the warning that he is the last in the line. This is, I think, what Jesus' eschatology is all about. Israel's history is drawing to its climax.

The events of 70 C.E. thus once again become significant in the argument. If the Romans do this (i.e., the crucifixion of Jesus) when the wood is green, what will they do when it is dry, when thousands of young Jews are crucified outside Jerusalem, guilty of the "crime" of which Jesus was innocent (Caird 1963:249–50; 1965:22;

Downing 1963)? But the question as to whether
Jesus preached judgment at all is itself one of the
many controversial areas in the Third Quest. Borg
thinks he did, and makes this fact central. Sanders
thinks he approved of John the Baptist's message
of judgment, but did not find it necessary to
repeat it (1985:322, 326). One aspect of Sanders'
book that I find strange at this point is his treatment of the Temple sayings. Though only one of
the sayings attributed to Jesus by the evangelists
even mentions the *rebuilding* of the Temple (John
2:16; the other sayings which mention this aspect
are put in the mouth of *false* witnesses), Sanders
passes very quickly over the overwhelmingly negative aspect of all the other sayings about the
Temple, and focuses attention instead on restoration as though this were the main explicit theme
(1985:71; Borg 1984: chap. 7).

These various levels in the discussion of eschatology reveal one final and vital feature of the
Jesus-and-Judaism discussion. It will not do to
drive a wedge between politics and theology,
between national and "eschatological" expectation. We cannot either insist *a priori* on a non-
political Jesus in order to reject revolutionary
reading, or expose the weaknesses in the revolutionary case and imagine that we have thereby
argued for a non-political Jesus. One of the great
merits of Borg's first book is its grasping of this
nettle. He explains that by "politics" he means "the
concern about the structure and purpose of a historic community." Jesus' message was addressed to
Israel, and

to be a religious figure in this tradition was
quite different from being a religious figure in
a tradition which defines religion as, for
example, what persons do with their solitude.
It meant to face questions about the purpose,
structure and destiny of the historic community of Israel. What did it mean to be the people
of God? In particular, in a setting in which
Israel's sovereignty was denied and her very
existence threatened by the imperial combination of Hellenistic culture and Roman military
power, what did it mean to be Israel, the people of promise destined to rule Yahweh's created order? (Borg 1984:3–4)

In such a world, to be non-political is to be irrelevant.

Borg's definition of "political" may still, however, be too wide for some. He shows, I think, that
Jesus is concerned with *society;* but, if "politics"
refers to the detailed mechanisms of actual power
("the science and art of government" is the definition offered by the *Concise Oxford Dictionary*), one
could still say either that Jesus held aloof from it
(he did not try to get himself appointed to the San-
hedrin), or, perhaps better, that he challenged the
whole power-system of first-century Israel by setting up himself and the twelve in a new and highly paradoxical position of *alternative* political
"power"–which turned out to redefine the meanings of both politics and power (Riches
1980:171–72). In this sense he was indeed "political": such an adjective by no means indicates
that one is underwriting anyone else's particular
program. We have seen in our own generation

what happens to those who refuse to run with the hares or hunt with the hounds. To tell all sides that their vision for the nation is wrong, and to act as if one has glimpsed, and is implementing, a different vision, is to invite trouble. The strength of this analysis, applied to Jesus, is that it makes him, as we said before, both comprehensible and crucifiable. Out of the morass of discussion in the Third Quest, an increasingly clear answer to the first question is emerging: Jesus cannot be separated from his Jewish context, but neither can he be collapsed into it so that he is left without a sharp critique of his contemporaries. I do my best to clarify and develop this insight throughout *Jesus and the Victory of God* (Wright 1996).

What Were Jesus' Aims?

The second question follows naturally from the first. What was Jesus seeking to *do* with Judaism? What event or sets of events would mean, from the perspective of his ministry, that he could say "I have succeeded in my aim"? From the viewpoint of conservative orthodoxy the answer would be "he aimed to die as a sacrifice for the sins of the world"; for Reimarus or Brandon, it would be "he aimed to liberate Jews from their Roman overlords." Granted that both of these, in different ways, are as they stand simplistic and misleading, how can we sketch an alternative that is not?

Was Jesus trying to change individuals, to change society, to change the world, or all of the above—and if so how? In particular, was his death accidental to the purpose of his life, or did he in any sense intend it? Theology has usually been content to jump from the question of why Jesus was born to the question of why he died, leaving the field clear for romantic or political reconstructions of the ministry. At best, some Catholic writing has suggested that his one aim was to found the church—which of course he did simply by calling the disciples (especially Peter), teaching them what they needed to know, and then dying for their sins. This solution has the merit that it tries to take the life of Jesus seriously from a theological point of view. It has the drawback, however, that it leaves the first of the five questions out of consideration, except in so far as it requires Judaism to be the dark backdrop against which all this could be understood. This problematic position must not remain unchallenged. Instead, we must stress the central importance of questions concerning Jesus' aims, desires, aspirations, and goals (Wright 1992a:110–11, 125–26).

An objection to this set of questions was lodged two generations ago by Cadbury (1962), who suggested that the whole idea of a person having consistent and life-directing aims was anachronistic. This, however, is spurious. Paul was clearly motivated by a long-held overarching aim, which he followed consistently. So, as far as we can tell, was John the Baptist. So were many figures in the Greco-Roman world about whom we have reliable information. Similarly, it has often been supposed that the intentions of human beings, not least in ancient history, are bound to be opaque to us. It is so hard to reconstruct what went on in somebody's head in another period of history, so impossible to be sure we have got it right. And yet this is in fact the stuff of which history is made. When we look for explanations of events in the world of human affairs, we are seeking for human motivations (Wright 1992a:109–12).

How may we go about this perilous search? How, in other words, may we engage in the full historical task? There are two things to look for in particular. First, we must study the *worldview* of the society or culture, or subculture, concerned. We must understand the way people looked at the world, what they hoped for, what they were afraid of. We can assume some continuity with other human societies with which we are more familiar, but we had better not assume too much. If, for instance, a future historian of the Second World War were to study the Japanese Kamikaze pilots, she would fail to understand the whole phenomenon unless she managed to get inside the worldview of the Japanese of that period, in which human life, including one's own, was counted cheap in comparison with the coming victory of the race as a whole—not an idea that would necessarily occur at once to a modern western historian. If, as another example, one tried to understand the Desert Fathers, one would have to get inside the whole worldview of early Egyptian Christianity. One could at no point presume that a transfer of ideas would be possible. If, finally, coming closer to our subject, we were to read the parable of the prodigal son without realizing that the son's initial request for his share of the inheritance would be "heard," within peasant village culture, as expressing the shocking wish that his father were dead, the entire reading of the parable would get off on the wrong foot (see Bailey 1983, vol. 1:161–69). We can only avoid such problems by painstaking historical and cultural research.

Second, we must study the *mindset* of the individual concerned. This will normally be a variation—sometimes a mutation—on the worldview as a whole. Worldviews themselves are necessarily large and overarching, and there is plenty of room for local and individual variation. Most human beings possess a mindset that retains a fair degree of consistency over time. Mavericks do arise, and people do odd things without—even to themselves—apparent motivation. But where an individual seems to have made up his or her mind on an issue, and be acting with a measure of consistency, in accordance with a particular plan (even if the actual plan remains opaque to onlookers), it makes sense to ask what it is that motivates that individual, what his or her particular aims may be. Moreover—and this is the point I wish to make here—this set of questions applies just as much in ancient as in modern history. We can ask, perfectly meaningfully, why Hannibal wanted to march on Rome, and why he chose to go the way he did. We can understand his mindset as a mutation of the regular Carthaginian one. We can ask, perfectly meaningfully, why Seneca committed suicide, and answer the question by reconstructing the worldview of Roman Stoics under Nero, and the particular mindset of Seneca himself as a variant or mutation of that worldview. There is nothing odd about this; it is actually what historians do all the time, though New Testament scholars often talk as if it were not. There is nothing in principle magical or mystical, nothing in principle inaccessible, about the settled intentions, aims, or ambitions of an individual. Even if little is said about them, they will gradually become apparent in actions performed, in choices made, in lifestyles adopted. In searching for the aims of Jesus, we are looking for a particular mindset within a particular worldview, quite possibly challenging that worldview in some ways, but with intentions that make sense in relation to it. This quest is in principle possible; I hope to show that it can be realized in practice.

What options have been offered on this question? The traditional pre-critical view was, as we have said, that Jesus came to die for the sins of the world, and/or to found the church. The Old Quest, by contrast, tended to assume—and this is still followed in much of the New Quest—that Jesus was basically a *teacher*: hence the concentration on his sayings, and the continual attempt to make them into timeless proclamation of truths about a god, or about human relationships. Jesus intended, on this view, to tell people something new, to impart information they did not previously possess. This viewpoint is still reflected in the work of Vermes. But most Third Quest writers have homed in on more specific aims, almost always taking for granted that Jesus' aims had to do with the kingdom, and proceeding from there. Thus we find that Jesus intended to foment revolution of one sort or another (Brandon and others); or, again, that he intended to oppose revolutionary zeal (Hengel, Borg). We read that Jesus intended to bring to birth the "restoration eschatology" that he, like some others, believed in, involving the destruction and rebuilding of the Temple (Sanders). Or, again, he intended to bring about a radical reform in the sacrificial cult of Jerusalem; only when this failed to come about did he alter his focus and regard his fellowship-meals with his followers as an *alternative* to the Temple (Chilton). Again, Jesus intended to establish a nexus between Israel and himself, such that Israel was already being restored in his words, his acts, and finally in his death (Meyer 1979:221–22, 251–53). Or Jesus intended to announce to Israel a new way of being the people of God, which would involve finding the way through vicarious suffering to the "vindication of the son of man," which would include the destruction of the Temple (Caird).

There are two interlocking questions that emerge from this brief survey. First, did Jesus remain true to one set of aims throughout his life, or did he change his mind at a particular stage? Second, did Jesus go up to Jerusalem with the intention of dying there? A third question, concerning Jesus' sense of personal vocation, is usually also waiting in the wings as these ones are under discussion.

There are various ways of postulating a change of mind. The classic form is that of Renan: the "Galilean springtime," in which Jesus is popular and successful, is followed by a cooler, and darker, period when it seems as though his demands are too heavy to be met. Subsequent forms of the theory include those of Buchanan (Jesus wanted to be a subversive revolutionary, and then changed his mind in order to go to the cross) and Chilton (Jesus wanted to reform the Temple and its sacrificial system; having failed, he treated his followers as a counter-Temple movement; see Buchanan 1984; Chilton 1992). The change of mind, clearly, relates directly to the second of the interlocking questions: did Jesus go to Jerusalem in order to die?

Schweitzer declared long ago that one could in fact divide up Lives of Jesus into two categories: did Jesus go to Jerusalem to work or to die? Schweitzer himself firmly took the latter option, though he too postulated a change of mind: Jesus did not originally intend to die, but to prepare the way for the victorious "coming of the son of man." It was only after the apparent failure of his mission—the failure of the son of man to appear—that he took it upon himself to force the divine hand. So, in a famous passage, Schweitzer saw Jesus putting into operation his revised aim (the added italics indicating where the change of mind occurred):

> In the knowledge that He is the coming Son of Man [Jesus] lays hold of the wheel of the world to set it moving on that last revolution which is to bring all ordinary history to a close. It *refuses to turn, and He throws Himself on it.* Then it does turn; and crushes Him. Instead of bringing in the eschatological conditions, He has destroyed them. The wheel rolls onward, and the mangled body of the one immeasurably great Man, who was strong enough to think of Himself as the spiritual ruler of mankind and to bend history to his purpose, is hanging upon it still. That is His victory and His reign. (Schweitzer 1954:368–69)

A softer version of this position is taken by Meyer: Jesus, having always reckoned with the possibility of violent death, built this more firmly into the structure of his aims quite early on in the course of the ministry (Meyer 1979:252; see also Schillebeeckx 1979:298–302; Witherington 1990:

262). Sanders pronounced this whole view, of Jesus going to Jerusalem to die, "weird" (1985:333); but this, I think, failed to take fully into account the major differences of worldview between first-century Palestine and modern America (Neyrey 1991:xiv and elsewhere). Moule, with a far more nuanced account, suggests that, although Jesus did not seek death, "he did pursue, with inflexible devotion, a way of truth that inevitably led him to death, and he did not seek to escape . . . He knew he was, in fact, bound to die, and he made no attempt either to escape or to defend himself" (Moule 1977:109, referring to John Downing 1963).

If we push both the options (going to work, or to die) into a more clear-cut form, we find the following antithesis. For Vermes, Jesus simply died in despair and with a broken heart, his life-aim in ruins (1993:207). For Caird, conversely, "not only in theological truth but in historic fact, the one bore the sins of the many, confident that in him the whole Jewish nation was being nailed to the cross, only to come to life again in a better resurrection" (1965:22). Thus the question, whether Jesus intended to die, and if so whether he gave his death any particular theological interpretation, remains firmly open within Third Quest study.

The further question, whether Jesus intended to found a church (or even *the* church), clearly needs more refinement. The question is often asked, and answered, with some scorn, on the assumption that, if the answer is "yes," we must think of Jesus envisaging cathedrals, cardinals, popes, processions, Archbishops of Canterbury, and all. Thus Vermes: "if [Jesus] meant and believed what he preached . . . namely that the eternal Kingdom of God was truly at hand, he simply could not have entertained the idea of founding and setting in motion an organized society intended to endure for ages to come (1993:214–15). If, however, we follow either Meyer or Sanders, and see Jesus' aim as the restoration, in some sense, of Israel, beginning with the highly symbolic call of twelve disciples, then the apparently peculiar idea of Jesus "founding" a community designed to outlast his death gives way to a more nuanced, and perfectly credible, first-century Jewish one: that of Jesus restoring the people of God, and doing so in some sense around himself. Anyone who cherished such a goal was *ipso facto* intending to leave behind a community, a renewed Israel, that would continue his work (so, for example, Lohfink 1984). One must assume that, by the same token, this was true of the Teacher of Righteousness, of Judas the Galilean, of Hillel and Shammai, and of the ill-fated Simeon ben Kosiba. This is a thoroughly Jewish intention, which cannot be dismissed by hinting sarcastically that one can hardly envisage Jesus envisaging the contemporary church.

A third question that is aroused by the wave of current study is, of course, whether Jesus' aims included a sense of personal vocation: in other words, whether he believed himself to possess a special role in the kingdom he was proclaiming. Again, the pre-critical idea that Jesus knew himself to be the divine Messiah was well and truly rejected in the Old Quest and, largely, in the New. The Third Quest has quite rightly separated out

the question of Messiahship from that of "divinity," focusing almost exclusively on the former.
Many Third Questers are happy to say that Jesus
saw himself as having a key role, probably the
Messianic role, within the divine purposes that he
aimed to put into operation. Harvey, scaling down
the meaning of "Christ" more than a little, is able
to conclude that Jesus was known by this title
during his lifetime (1982:80–82, 120–51). Sanders
regards it as "highly probable" that "Jesus' disciples thought of him as 'king,'" and that he accept-
ed the role, either implicitly or explicitly
(1985:234, 321, 326). Witherington goes further
still: Jesus clearly believed himself to be Messiah
(1990:267-75). At the same time, of course, there
are still plenty who stand firm on the older view,
that Jesus saw himself, at most, as a prophet (Vermes 1973). We have come a long way from
Wrede's shallow identification of Messianic status
with a heavenly son of man figure and with the
later Christian claim about Jesus' "divinity." But
we are still a long way from agreement.

What then did Jesus aim to do, and how did
this work out in specific intentions? The answer,
from within most of the Third Quest, seems to
have something to do with the kingdom; something to do with the Temple; something to do with
Jesus himself; just possibly something to do with
his death; conceivably something to do with a
group of people continuing his work after his
death. Can we move further? I argue that we can.
In each case, of course, we meet a further form of
the familiar problem: since the first generation of
Jesus' followers regarded themselves as in some

senses continuing his work and mission, and as in some sense the heirs of his teaching and actions, and the beneficiaries of his death, it is natural that they would tell stories about him which made it appear that he had indeed intended all of this. If the stories provide the legitimation for aspects of the early church, how can we trust them to tell us about Jesus? This problem can, however, be resolved, in principle at least, by the resolute pursuit of a serious historical hypothesis about Jesus himself. Otherwise, "critical history" becomes mere paranoia, insisting on conspiracy theories and unable to see the way that the real evidence is pointing.

The question of Jesus' aims, therefore, is nowhere near as simple as either pre-critical Christianity thought, or as some within the various Quests have imagined. There are several avenues of inquiry that the question opens up; and we cannot retreat from them as though there were nothing much more to be said. Out of the many lines that positively demand to be pursued at this point, there is one in particular to which all these questions point forward, and with which they are all significantly integrated. This is the next major question to be addressed: why did Jesus die?

Why Did Jesus Die?

Whether or not one concludes that Jesus himself intended to die, it does not follow that this intention was a sufficient cause of his crucifixion. Ignatius fully intended to die as a martyr, but envisaged the possibility that meddling Christians in Rome might prevent him (Ign. *Rom.* 2). Paul knew he might well be called upon to face execution, but kept an open mind about whether and when this would come to pass (Phil 1:20-26; and 1 Thess 4:17; 1 Cor 15:51; 2 Cor 1:9; 4:16–5:10). Even if we take the strong view that Jesus fully intended to die, and that he invested this death, in advance, with some sort of theological interpretation, we still need to know what the Romans thought they were doing when they crucified him. Granted that they crucified quite a lot of people, it is still only the extreme historical skeptic who will suggest that there was anything random or accidental about their execution of Jesus.

What, then, were the circumstances that led to this event? What were the aims and intentions, expressive of worldviews and mindsets, of the various actors involved? At this level, of course, the question is on a par with other (comparatively) straightforward questions: why did John the Baptist die? Why did Julius Caesar die? And, if we wish to include cases in which the subject's own intentionality was clearly involved, why did Seneca die? Why did Ignatius die? Why did Eleazar, the leader of the Sicarii on Masada, die? These rough parallels demonstrate that, though it is of course difficult, the question can in principle be addressed by regular historical means.

This historical question, searching for the human motivations that led to Jesus' death, has regularly been confused with a quite different one. "Why did Jesus die?" if asked in many Christian circles, would elicit a range of "theological" answers: he died for the sins of the world, to defeat the devil, to save people from eternal death, or whatever. The two sorts of answers appear to be in watertight compartments. The evangelists only hint at an answer of the second type (the theological), and appear to concentrate on the first (the historical); it is thus often assumed that they do not have what is called a "theology of the cross"—though it has also been held that their apparent "history" is fairly worthless, precisely because it reads the theological viewpoint of the church back into the narrative! For these reasons, it is vital that we inquire carefully what precisely an "historical" explanation of the cross might consist in, and that we then attempt to offer exactly that. In other words, we must entertain the serious possibility that the "theological" accounts of the crucifixion that we find in early and subsequent Christianity—already, for instance, in Paul—may have nothing to do with what actually happened; and also that the apparently "historical" accounts of the evangelists are themselves the reading back of later theological, or even political, interests. This third question is thus very firmly set within the overall historical task of *Jesus and the Victory of God*.

What, then, is the range of possible answers to the third question, at a "historical" level? One obvious answer, given among Jews from at least the time of the Talmud, is that Jesus died because he was perceived as a deceiver of the people. Another, given among historians since at least the time of Reimarus, is that he was executed simply because he was a revolutionary. Jesus, in other words, clearly offended either official Israel or official Rome, possibly both. But the long and tragic legacy of anti-semitism within a self-styled Christian culture has meant that scholars are now rightly sensitive about even appearing to say "the Jews crucified Jesus"; and the pressure of historical evidence has led almost all scholars to doubt whether Jesus was in fact executed by the Romans on a straightforward, and manifestly deserved, charge of stirring up sedition (Harvey 1982: chap. 2; Brown 1994). The old views, that Jews espoused a corrupt form of religion and therefore hated Jesus for preaching a better one, and that Jesus posed a straightforward revolutionary threat to (Roman) public order, are to be rejected (see Sanders 1985:296–306, 331). Someone, or more likely some group, wanted Jesus out of the way for somewhat less obvious reasons.

But what were those reasons? That there was a "political" element to it—in other words, that the Romans were convinced, or at least persuaded, that Jesus was some sort of a troublemaker—seems clear. But who convinced, or persuaded, them? Here there have been two mainstream alternatives: the Pharisees, and the Temple hierarchy. It used to be thought that Jesus' clashes with the Pharisees, as recorded in the synoptic tradition (e.g., Mark 2:23–3:6), consisted of his standing up against the "petty legalism" of the Pharisees; that they reacted, to protect their own interests, by plotting against him; that these plots reached a crescendo, culminating in Jesus' trial before Jewish authorities; and that this essentially "religious" charge was then turned neatly into a "political" one, enabling him to be handed over to the pagans. This produces an answer to the question that purchases its clarity (Jesus constantly provokes the Pharisees to kill him, which they eventually succeed in doing) at the cost of historical plausibility. There is no historical verisimilitude in the picture of the Pharisees as petty, and perhaps Pelagian, legalists. There is no evidence that the Pharisees as such were directly involved in the events which led to Jesus' actual death. And there is no connection, in this scheme, between the Pharisees' reaction to Jesus and the Temple incident, which looms so large in the narratives leading to the crucifixion.

Against this simplistic line, Sanders in particular has argued that Jesus probably never disputed with the Pharisees anyway; that it was his action in the Temple which caused all the trouble; that those who were offended by this action, and who responded by (somehow) handing him over to the Romans, were not Pharisees at all, but were the chief priests and rulers (Sanders 1985:309–18; Vermes 1973:36–37). This reaction, though perhaps necessary, has in my judgment gone too far. Many serious scholars still hold out for Jesus having had serious disputes with the Pharisees. But to argue for a third, quite different, position will take some little while (see Wright 1996: 540–611). Once again, however, we may note that in the Third Quest one particular strand is emerging as vital and central, namely Jesus' attitude to the Temple, and the possible connection of that with his death. Chilton, indeed, argues that what Judas betrayed, and what Jesus was crucified for, was not his action in the Temple but his regarding of himself and his followers as a counter-Temple movement (1992:150–55); but this simply confirms the current tendency, which I believe to be profoundly correct, to associate the Temple with Jesus' death. The precise nature of that association, however, must remain for the moment *sub judice* (not yet decided).

There is still, of course, the question of the "trial" which Jesus may have undergone. In the synoptic tradition, this consists of a hearing before the chief priests, followed by a hearing before the governor, Pilate. Most recent scholars who have discussed these narratives have expressed considerable skepticism; once again the shadow of anti-semitism rears up, as various writers do their best to exonerate "the Jews" from any complicity whatever in Jesus' death. The various questions this has raised in turn (whether the Jewish authorities had the right to execute people; whether the "trial" before the high priest could have taken place according to Jewish law; whether there was a charge of "blasphemy" leveled at Jesus, etc.) have been debated this way and that without any of the issues being resolved. Nevertheless, in so far as there is any consensus within the Third Quest at the moment, it is that Jesus was handed over to the pagan rulers by the official Jewish authorities. Clearly there remains a good deal of work to do in this area if we are to give the third question anything like a clear answer.

If we manage, by whatever means, to arrive at a satisfactory answer to the historical question as to why Jesus died, there remains still the theological question. This forces itself upon the historian, willy-nilly, because very early within the Christian tradition a theological interpretation was given to Jesus' death. "Christ died *for our sins*" was already a traditional formula within a few years of the crucifixion; Paul could write not long afterwards that "the son of God loved me and gave himself for me" (1 Cor 15:3 [quoting a very early formula]; Gal 2:20). Part of the explanation for Jesus' death, therefore, must include its sequel: why did the early church come to attach to Jesus' execution such far-reaching significance? This, however, already trespasses on the territory of the fourth major question.

How and Why Did the Early Church Begin?

The understanding of any event is not only bound to involve, but may well be enhanced by, the understanding of its sequel. Thus (for instance) one of the merits of Sanders' work is that he reasons backwards from the fact that, after Jesus' death, the disciples were not, as one might have expected, rounded up and arrested, and perhaps executed, in their turn. But, as well as negative arguments such as this, there are positive questions: what (if anything) actually happened on Easter morning? Like Bach's Passion music, the current studies of Jesus are perfectly valid even if, like *Jesus and the Victory of God,* they come to a halt on Good Friday. But the Third Quest cannot for that reason put off forever the question of the resurrection. I shall return to it myself in due course.

Nor can it escape from the (perfectly virtuous) circle of (a) studying Jesus in the light of the Gospels, and hence of the early church, and (b) studying the early church, including the Gospels, in the light of Jesus. Hypotheses at the one point have to dovetail, and routinely within the discipline do dovetail, with hypotheses at the other point. That is why I spent five chapters of *The New Testament and the People of God* discussing the early church and the Gospels as arising within it. But the question now before us focuses quite narrowly on one particular moment. I argued earlier that:

> What united early Christians, deeper than all diversity, was that they told, and lived, a form of Israel's story that reached its climax in Jesus and then issued in their spirit-given new life and task. . . .
>
> The church appropriated for itself the Jewish belief that the creator God would rescue his people at the last, and interpreted that rescue in terms of a great lawcourt scene . . . The major underlying difference between the Christian and the Jewish views at this point was that the early Christians believed that the verdict had already been announced in the death and resurrection of Jesus. . . .
>
> First-century Jews looked forward to a public event . . . in and through which their God would reveal to all the world that he was not just a local, tribal deity, but the creator and sovereign of all. . . . The early Christians . . . looked back to an event in and through which, they claimed, Israel's God had done exactly that. (Wright 1992a:456, 458, 476)

How, as historians, are we to describe this event, which resulted in the church believing that the eschaton had now arrived, but which was not itself the eschaton as they had imagined it? Though this question has not been seriously addressed within Third Quest studies, there are several pointers to it. This is perhaps clearest in the work of Sanders: "Without the resurrection, would [Jesus'] disciples have endured longer than did John the Baptist's? We can only guess, but I would guess not" (1985:240). So would I. One might add, for good measure, the followers not only of John the Baptist but of Judas the Galilean, Simon, Athronges, Eleazar ben Deinaus and Alexander, Menahem, Simon bar Giora, and bar-Kochba himself (Wright 1992a:170–81). Faced with the defeat of their leader, followers of such figures would either be rounded up as well or melt away into the undergrowth. The other possibility was to latch on to a new leader: in the case of the apparent dynasty that ended up being known as the Sicarii, when one leader was killed they simply chose another from the same family. In not one case do we hear of any group, after the death of its leader, claiming that he was in any sense alive again, and that therefore Israel's expectation had in some strange way actually come true. History therefore spotlights the question: What happened to make Jesus' followers, from the very start, articulate such a claim and work out its implications? Sanders again:

> We have every reason to think that Jesus had led [the disciples] to expect a dramatic event which would establish the kingdom. The death and resurrection required them to adjust their expectation, but did not create a new one out of nothing. (1985:320)

Again, I totally agree; but what content do we then give to the resurrection itself? Here Sanders leaves the argument pointing forward towards the key question, but without addressing it: "[Jesus'] followers, by carrying through the logic of his own position *in a transformed situation,* created a movement which would grow and continue to alter . . ." (1985:340, italics added). Quite so. But what changed the situation?

If the question of the origin of the early church thus pushes us relentlessly back toward the problem of Easter, the same question broadens out to include all sorts of features that appear in the early church, claiming continuity of some sort with Jesus himself. Thus we must ask: why and how did the early disciples, shattered as they had been by the crucifixion of their master, regroup and go out to face persecution for declaring that in him the hope of Israel had quite literally come to life? Why did they then organize themselves and act in the way that they did, and, in particular, why (granted their abiding commitment to Jewish-style monotheism) did they begin very early on to *worship* Jesus, and to include him in Jewish-style monotheistic formulae (Wright 1992a:362, 448; 1991:chaps. 4–6; also Hurtado 1988; Bauckham 1992)? Why did their communities take the form they did, which as it turns out was very different from any of the standard models available in the ancient world, being neither an ethnic group worshipping a tribal deity nor a private religious club? So different was it, after all, that the early Christians sometimes had to argue to the authorities, against apparent appearances, that they were in some sense or other a "religious" organization. It was perhaps almost as much their socio-cultural oddness as their denial of the pagan deities that earned them the title "atheists." There were no other groups in the ancient world going around claiming to *be* the human race (I owe this whole point to Bishop

Rowan Williams). And, since the answer the early Christians themselves seem to have given to the question has to do both with Jesus of Nazareth prior to his death and with their belief that he had been raised from the dead, the historian is bound to ask whether we are forced to reject either of these answers. If, for instance, the Q community—supposing there to have been such a thing—was composed of wandering radicals, from whom did they get the idea? And why did they still think it worth pursuing after Jesus' death?

The impetus towards including this fourth question within the study of Jesus comes partly from the sense of incompleteness (both historical and theological) that may be felt when some of the current quest is reviewed. Some of the pieces of the jigsaw appear to be still in the box; studying the sequel to the event may perhaps bring them to light. Some of the Third Quest authors, implicitly addressing these questions, have to postulate a large gap between Jesus and the early church; having located Jesus, supposedly, within his native Judaism, they have the early church located nowhere in particular, certainly not in any very direct connection to Jesus. I will aim to avoid such a *prima facie* weakness (the reverse, more or less, of Bultmann's), and to demonstrate, at least preliminarily, the continuity, as well as the clear discontinuities, between Jesus and the early church.

All pictures of Jesus, then, depend to a lesser or greater extent on a complementary picture of the early church. Again we are faced with the problem of the interrelation of history and theology. In the standard Bultmannian paradigm the history of the early church (as opposed to the history of

Jesus) provided the context and explanation for the rise of particular theological beliefs. Some of these were then regarded as valid, either because of their history-of-religious pedigree, or because they cohered with some other external standard. I hope I shall be spared to address this whole problem, which I regard as urgent, not only theologically but also historically.

Why Are the Gospels What They Are?

It is a commonplace of Gospel study that we have in Matthew, Mark, and Luke a new genre of literature. It is not quite this and not quite that; neither simply biography nor simply religious propaganda, yet sharing the main characteristics of both. No one is quite sure how to account for this genre, but there it is. And yet the Gospels clearly stand in some sort of relation to Jesus himself, and their existence is in some way or other derived from what he was and did and said. Why, then, are they what they are? This question is of course a subset of the previous one, but it is so specialized as to be worth setting out on its own, without forgetting its links with what has preceded. With this question, in fact, we have reached the other side of the jigsaw whose central piece is Jesus. First-century Judaism and the Gospels are opposite edges, and all discourse about Jesus must take place between them. One can thus see at a glance the reason for the complexity of such discourse, since both edges are themselves so difficult to describe accurately and hence to work within. Answering this fifth question will take at least a whole book. But it will be an enormous strength for any hypothesis about Jesus if it can at least indicate why, if Jesus was as the hypothesis suggests, the Gospels are what they are.

The Five Questions Together

It should be noted once more that the five questions fit together very closely, so that answers to any of them have repercussions elsewhere. It is comparatively easy to find an answer to one of them, but fitting it with answers to the rest is not. Together they form the jigsaw of Jesus himself, which is itself a piece in the larger jigsaw of the rise of Christianity as a whole. The five questions can, in fact, be drawn together under two headings: Jesus' relation to Judaism on the one hand and to the early church on the other (Neill and Wright 1988:398–401).

Different schools of thought have emphasized one or another question and ignored the rest; sometimes the solution advanced to one has meant a particularly awkward and ill-fitting answer to the others. Wrede and Schweitzer, once again, provide paradigms: Wrede analyzed Jesus in a fairly minimal way, and in consequence put a good deal of weight first on the early church and then on the Gospels. Schweitzer's apocalyptic Jesus generated an apocalyptic early church—including Paul and the Gospels—which nevertheless can be seen as the beginning of the later, wider, Hellenistic developments.

Perhaps the best example of the integration of the questions, in terms of twentieth-century scholarship, is Rudolf Bultmann. Bultmann put all the weight on Question 4 (the rise of the early church). The early church began with a tremendous burst of creative energy, finding, in the

proclamation of the crucified Jesus as the living
Lord, the key to unlock the prison of human existence. It expressed this faith in language that, to
the untrained eye, can be mistakenly thought to
refer to Jesus, but which in fact is, strictly,
"mythological," i.e., a projection on to "history"
of the present experience of "faith." This view,
however, has grave difficulties with Questions
1–3. Jesus is not really related to Judaism at all,
except by a contrast of abstract ideals; his own
aims were extremely generalized and only mar-
ginally related to the concerns of most Jews of
his day; the historical reasons for his death,
which are in any case hidden from us, have nothing whatever to do with the theological interpretation which the early church gave that event.
Question 5 also causes problems. Within the
usual form-critical paradigm, the evangelists
were simply collectors of stories that they strung
together without much regard for sequence. But
redaction criticism and subsequent literary critical study of the Gospels have cut off this branch
(although some redaction critics, perhaps out of
deference to their scholarly tradition, still claim
to be sitting on it). The Gospels are revealed as
quite sophisticated documents, and if we wish to
retain the Bultmannian paradigm we must invent
ever more cunning sub-theories to account for
them as they actually are. The great irony of this
total position, seen from the perspective I
advance in Wright 1996, is that it regards genuinely mythological language (apocalyptic) as
though it were understood "literally" by those
who first used it, and regards genuinely literal
language (talk about Jesus) as though it were

intended "mythologically" by those who first used it (Wright 1992a:297).

Within the Bultmannian scheme, and within the New Quest that retained at least some of his framework, critical methods became a means of maintaining a discreet reticence, or even silence, about Jesus, in the face of the threat that history might undermine faith (or, in the case of the "Jesus Seminar," the threat that history might somehow create or support orthodox faith). And, as we have seen, the emphasis on the history of the early church has led to ever more detailed, and unprovable, speculative hypotheses in the realm of tradition criticism. Such exercises would only be valuable if we knew a lot more about the early church than we actually do. Remythologization has replaced demythologization. The Bultmann school still needs history—but this time it is the history of the early church. And this requires a far greater effort of unsupported imagination from the historian than even the old liberal "lives" of Jesus did. Starting with an apparently solid answer to Question 4 has ended up in a cul-de-sac.

Just to be even-handed to the "giants," we may point out there that Schweitzer's theory is weakest, ironically, where it claimed to be strongest, i.e., in its treatment of Question 1. It is not at all clear that there ever was such a thing as the "late-Jewish apocalyptic worldview" upon which Schweitzer built so much (Schweitzer 1954: 364–68; Wright 1992a:333–34). He was right to insist on putting Jesus into his Jewish context; right to see that context as inescapably apocalyptic; but wrong to interpret that apocalyptic eschatology in the way

he did. This weakness is the fatal flaw that ultimately vitiates his fascinating answers to Questions 2 and 3, and calls his answers to 4 and 5 into
question as well.

It is a residual weakness even within the Third
Quest that one or other question tends to be highlighted at the expense of the rest. This does not (in
my view) result in such a dramatic failure as that
of Bultmann, but it still needs to be addressed. The
attempt to answer Questions 1 and 2 (Jesus' aims)
has sometimes resulted, as we have seen, in a picture of Jesus the revolutionary, whether military
(Brandon, Buchanan) or social (Horsley); this
never really comes to grips with Questions 4 and
5 (the church and the Gospels), except in terms of
a massive failure of nerve, or at least a total
change of direction, on the part of the early
church. And, since we only know about Questions
1–3 (the supposed strengths of such a view)
through the Gospels, which are the subject of question 5 and grow out of the early church discussed
in Question 4, the theories seem once more to be
sitting on branches that are mostly sawn through.
Vermes' picture of Jesus the Hasid (his answer to
Questions 1 and 2) fails altogether to explain why
Jesus was crucified (Question 3), and only
explains the rise of the early church (Question 4)
by an enormous leap into a religion completely
different from that of Jesus. By the content of his
very thorough answer to the first two questions, he
has made it very difficult to answer 3 at all, and
has been forced to produce very strained answers
to 4 and 5. Conversely, F. G. Downing has offered
a provocative and fascinating study of Jesus as a
Cynic preacher, which achieves its new angle on

Question 2 (Jesus' aims), and possible implicit solution to 3 (his death), at the enormous cost of an all-but-incredible answer to Question 1 (his relation to Judaism), and a failure to explain 4 (the church) and 5 (the Gospels) except, again, as a massive about-face. Horsley offers an answer to Question 2 (Jesus' aims), and to some extent 1 (his relation to Judaism), which make 3, 4 and 5 somewhat difficult: it is not clear from his book why Horsley's Jesus got crucified, or why the church would have taken the line, and written the books, that it did. Freyne addresses 1 and 5 superbly: his social history of Galilee, and his sensitive reading of the Gospels, is exemplary. But his placing of Jesus and the earliest Christians into his framework—his answer, in other words, to Questions 2, 3 and 4—is as yet not full enough to do justice to the complex issues involved (Freyne 1988; Horsley has now written about Jesus' death [1994]).

Among the other prominent Third Quest writers, Harvey's stated historical method insists on the primacy of placing Jesus within the "constraints" of his own time and setting. This, clearly, is a way of addressing the first two questions. He nevertheless, in my judgment, never totally takes on board the subtleties of the Jewish context and Jesus' aims in relation to it. He has an extensive explanation of the crucifixion (Question 3), which nevertheless does not explain why the early church came to give it the significance it did (i.e., the point at which Questions 3 and 4 overlap and interact). Why, in other words, did the early church move so quickly from their leader's execution to the belief that his death was "for our sins"? Harvey likewise never, at least in his book on

Jesus, addresses Question 5. Borg's reconstruction of Jesus' aims within his Jewish setting provides a fascinating and inviting set of answers to Questions 1 and 2. But he does not directly address Questions 3, 4, or 5; I find his indirect statements in these areas as yet unsatisfactory; though I believe that this is partly because he has not followed through his earlier arguments (in his 1984 book) as far as they will go. Sanders, who sees as clearly as anyone what the issues are, explicitly disavows "theological" interest, and thus avoids the challenge of integrating what happened in Jesus' ministry and death with the question of what the early church came to believe, and how they began to live and worship, after his death. In particular, as we saw, he avoids the sharp edge of Question 4 (the rise of the early church), by referring simply to "a changed situation." Borg and Sanders, despite their clear intention of answering Question 1 as fully as they can, never really get to grips with the first-century Jewish reading of Daniel 7 which forms an essential part of the background. Borg persists with the view—which originates in a period in which Question 1 was answered quite differently!—that Messiahship was not a major category for Jesus.

Meyer, whose major book is one of the most learned, patient and methodologically thorough of any in the last fifteen years—perhaps in the last 150—has likewise seen clearly the full range of issues. His reading of the Jewish context is sensitive, and his outlining of Jesus' aims well nuanced; his understanding of the cross goes far further than most other Third Quest writers. I find his accounts of Jesus' apocalyptic eschatology, and of the early church, less satisfying. At each point, despite my admiration for his work, I suggest possible improvements to his overall solution (Wright 1996).

The Sixth Question: Agenda and Theology

There is, of course, a sixth question, always in mind although different in character. How does the Jesus we discover by doing "history" relate to the contemporary church and world? This question cannot ultimately be bracketed out, though it is assumed here that it cannot be allowed to exercise leverage over the course of historical study. As we saw in *The New Testament and the People of God,* all history is of course a dialogue between student and sources, not a positivist's fantasy in which a "purely objective" point of view is attained by an observer who is, for the purposes of the argument, a negligible mathematical point. This does not mean, however, that the observer is allowed to inflict his or her point of view on to unwilling material. If the dialogue is to be an exercise in real history, the observer has to be prepared to change his or her mind. Instead of the spurious antithesis between "objective" and "subjective," we must hold to the proper distinction between public and private. We can debate in public; if we refuse to do so, we are left with private opinion. The historian is committed to working in public. If the historian is also committed in whatever sense, to living in some sort of continuity with certain features of the past, that of course gives to the whole exercise a peculiar sense of risk; but it should not mean that the historical task is reduced to terms of the historian's own antecedent beliefs or worldview.

There are, of course, huge issues at stake here. One of the major reasons for dialectical theology's refusal to continue the Old Quest was the belief that historical research would be of no theological use. The prodigal (Enlightenment historiography) is not welcome within the ancestral home. To put it bluntly, if one locates Jesus in first-century Palestine, one risks the possibility that he might have little to say to twentieth-century Europe, America or anywhere else—except, of course, by happy, or maybe contrived, coincidence. We have already seen how Schweitzer and Bultmann got round this problem. It was not a problem for the New Quest, since the hermeneutical and theological answers were implicitly built-in to it from the start: The Gospels became "meaningful" by various means, of which form and redaction criticism were but two.

The Third Quest has no predetermined route to follow here. That is just as well, if it is to retain its status as a major public enterprise, instead of collapsing (as the renewed New Quest is in danger of doing) into a private game. This is not to say that various Third Questers have not tried their hand at stating the results of their work for contemporary reflection. Harvey hints at a preacher's answer which he does not develop: The challenge of Jesus to his contemporaries "is capable of being presented with as much force today as it ever has been in the past" (Harvey 1982:173). Meyer hints at a Catholic solution: "it is above all in the tradition generated by Jesus that we discover what made him operate in the way he did, what made him epitomize his life in the single act of going to his death" (1979:252–53). Sanders boldly confronts would-be interpreters, telling them that if the history is done right the theology will look after itself. His own frequent mocking of various theological positions, however, leads one quickly to the conclusion, which he eventually confirms, that he has his own theological position (that of "a liberal, modern, secularized Protestant"), and that, even if Jesus did not die for this position, he certainly lived up to it (Sanders 1985:334; see the criticisms in Charlesworth 1988:28–29). Vermes, who protests too much in his "historian's reading of the Gospels," ends up with Jesus as (in the title of Henry Chadwick's BBC Radio 3 review when the book came out) "a rather pale Galilean," whose significance for today is not least that the church since Paul and John has, in "divinizing" him, radically misunderstood him (Vermes 1993:208–15). Some (Horsley, Downing, Mack) have thinly disguised social agendas which, worked out in terms of first-century Palestine, have clear implications for the modern world, but little to say about theology as such. Reading between the lines of Borg's main book one may hear a more subtle theme: Jesus' challenge to his contemporaries was a call to abandon nationalist or militarist political aspirations, and to imitate God in being merciful, rather than in maintaining a dualistic separation from the wicked world.

Such implications have not been discussed very explicitly or thoroughly within the Third Quest (but see Harvey 1990). This should not be taken to imply that this wave of studies has after all achieved "neutral" or "objective" results. One does not have to look very far beneath the surface to discover all sorts of implicit conclusions and rec-

ommendations. For Horsley, Jesus is on the side of
at least a moderate revolution. For Meyer, Jesus
points forward cryptically to something like mainstream Christianity (Meyer 1979:253). Even those
who (like Sanders and Vermes) claim to avoid theology reach conclusions which, as they very well
know, present a challenge to a number of different
theological positions, including those formerly
held by those two scholars themselves. They are as
aware as anyone of ways in which their work could
affect the way people actually think and behave in
the modern world (Vermes 1993:214–15). Since
the Third Quest has, in my opinion, a better chance
than any of its predecessors of achieving solid
answers to the five main questions about Jesus, it
is important that in concluding this chapter we
should explore where some of the theological and
practical possibilities may lie.

The first and sometimes most noticeable feature here is the use being made of answers to
Question 1, that is, of Jesus' relation to Judaism.
One of the initial impulses (not the only one)
towards the Third Quest has, I suspect, been the
desire to make Jesus more Jewish; this has been
reflected in a tendency towards a rather self-con-
scious philo-semitism. The incoming tide of post-
holocaust reaction has reached the study of Jesus.
The Pharisees were not, after all, the hardened
legalists of Matthew's Gospel, and they did not
engage in controversy with Jesus (Sanders). Jesus
did not teach, or believe, his own Messiahship, for
so long a stumbling-block to Jews: so Vermes, with
Bultmann (but for very different reasons) on his
side. The "constraint of monotheism" meant that
Jesus could not have thought of himself as divine,

but only as "son of God" in the sense of the accredited agent of the one God (Harvey). Rivkin's theological axe-grinding is the most marked: the blurb on the cover makes no pretense about neutral historical scholarship, but hails the book as "an important bridge of reconciliation between Jews and Christians." (I hope that *Jesus and the Victory of God* is that too; the serious search for historical foundations cannot but be healthy and air-clearing.) One of the notable features in some of the books I have listed is thus a response— sometimes implicit, sometimes loud and clear—to the charges of anti-semitism laid at the door of Christianity by a whole line of writers (for an obvious example, see Ruether 1974).

In the Jewish writers (Vermes, Rivkin) this comes across as an attempt, in line with earlier writers such as Klausner (1945), to reclaim Jesus. In some of the Christian writers (Harvey, Sanders) the implication (reading between the lines, in good form-critical manner) is one of contrition. Borg's striking thesis manages to have Jesus oppose the main lines of first-century Jewish aspirations without giving off the unpleasant odor of anti-Judaism, since he takes care to show that Jesus grounded his critique in mainstream, Jewish traditions rooted in the Hebrew scriptures. Riches, albeit armed with much modern learning, leans more towards an old-fashioned, almost an Old Quest, view of Judaism as a religion of judgment, in contrast with which Jesus taught a religion of mercy.

It is important to see this variety of positions on the question of the significance of Jesus' relation to Judaism not just as a series of knee-jerk reactions from different theological standpoints, but as part of a wider problem. The early years of this century saw history-of-religions research being conducted among Christians on the principle that Judaism was merely the dark background against which the bright light had shone, so that if Christianity wanted reputable ancestry it had better look elsewhere. The post-war reaction, in line with Barthian neo-orthodoxy, took the opposite line: Jewish ideas were "good," non-Jewish ones "bad." We are now at an interesting point of possible advance. What if (a) it is in fact much harder to distinguish between Jewish and non-Jewish ideas than used to be thought, and (b) we reject the belief that one can evaluate ideas by associating them with one culture or the other? The Third Quest has come to birth at a period of methodological indecision on such matters, and a variety of approaches is hardly surprising. But further progress it not to be expected unless the issue if squarely faced. Otherwise we will merely witness shadow-boxing, with historical argument as a cover for contemporary theologizing. That would reduce the present quest to the lowest level ever reached by its predecessors.

Probably the most sensitive theological issue to be discovered within the Third Quest, and certainly the one on which many will focus instant attention, is Christology. Is it possible to proceed, by way of historical study, to a portrait of Jesus which is sufficient of itself to evoke, or at least legitimate, that worship which Christianity has traditionally offered to him? If not, is this because we merely lack sufficient biographical information, or because we know *a priori* that anything in the Gospel accounts which might seem to present Jesus as worthy of worship must, for that reason if no other, be reckoned a later accretion? And, in the light of answers to these questions, how do we view the church's continuing use of the Gospels? Do we read them to find out more about Jesus "as he really was," or to reinforce the faith of the Gospel writers that, no matter who or what Jesus was in his earthly life, he is in fact the incarnate son of God, who died for us? Can these two levels of reading be combined, or are they mutually self-contradictory?

Three recent attempts to write about Jesus have offered ways in which history may be thought to lead to a positive christological conclusion. We saw earlier that Edward Schillebeeckx, at the end of his massive work, declares that he chooses to say, "Jesus is the Son of God." It may be doubted, however, whether the argument of the book actually leads to this conclusion. It seems that Schillebeeckx himself has merely jumped from a complex historical thesis to a theological judgment without any visible connection between the two. Anthony Harvey, in his briefer and more stimulating work, speaks of an historical inquiry, for which materials are now available,

> which will enable us to understand better what it might mean to claim that "God was with" a person of history in such a unique and decisive way that he could be regarded as an actual agent of the divine, and become thereby an object, not only of our endless and fascinated study, but of our love and worship. (1982:10)

Again, it maybe doubted whether Harvey has produced an argument that will carry all his readers with him. But the attempt to move from Jesus to christology calls for further reflection. (Such an attempt–not, I think, wholly successful–may be seen in Fredriksen 1988.) Witherington, having argued in detail that Jesus believed himself to be Messiah, opts for a cautious but open-ended possibility: that Jesus saw himself "not merely as a greater king than David but in a higher and more transcendent category" (1990:276). A lot more work is clearly required if such questions are to be addressed satisfactorily.

Though several of the practitioners of the Third Quest (e.g., Sanders) leave the christological question more or less explicitly out of consideration, it cannot in fact be put off for ever, and *Jesus and the Victory of God* attempts to address it head on. The Third Quest may look, to some suspicious eyes, as though it is bound to end up with an old-fashioned "liberal" Jesus, really just a human being and nothing more. From the other end of the telescope, of course, anything that *did* end up with an argument, based on history, that showed a continuous line between Jesus' own understanding of himself and the early church's high Christology would be at once, for that very reason, suspect in many quarters. But, if we play the game properly– if, that is, we leave the meanings of "divine" and "human" as unknowns until we have looked at the material–then there can be no advance prediction of what the result may look like (Wright 1992a: xiv–xv, 12, 248–59, 456–58, 471–76).

Future Directions of the Third Quest

Where, then, is the Third Quest going? Some of its practitioners, it seems, are similar in outlook to Reimarus: if we study the history for all it is worth, we shall find that Christian theology can safely be downgraded. Others are more like some of the Old Questers: we must integrate a historical portrait of Jesus with a rediscovery of his religious significance. I wish to share the concern of the former for rigorous historical construction, and also to work towards a new integration of history and theology which will do justice, rather than violence, to both. The Third Quest has produced tools that enable us to attempt this task with high hopes.

There will, of course, be varied reactions to the Third Quest in general. Many will echo the reaction of dialectical theology to the Old Quest and to Schweitzer himself: give us something of instant use for theology, or we shall declare your work irrelevant (Morgan 1987). The older brother is not going to like it if the prodigal tries to come back home. Old memories die hard; Reimarus' revolutionary Jesus, Schweitzer's apocalyptic visionary, and Vermes' Galilean Hasid have all caused consternation among theologians. One might even foresee a new "demythologization" program, designed to free Jesus from the political entanglements which Horsley and others get him into, just as Bultmann's program tried to liberate him from Jewish apocalyptic thought. One can certainly foresee that many will take what is useful to them from the current debate and fit it into a framework of their own devising, however inappropriately; this disease is endemic to scholarship, my own no doubt included, and there is no reason to imagine that the present wave of studies will be exempt. Nor is this problem confined to those who want to find a Jesus on whom they can base their own brand of faith. Others are just as good at finding a Jesus on whom they can base their own brand of agnosticism. But we should not be put off from undertaking, and advancing, the Third Quest by the fears of those who say it will be useless for the practice or the theology of the church. (Sometimes, of course, this simply means that it will prove too challenging, and so is to be left aside.) Having lived with this dilemma for several years, I am convinced that the way out is forward, not backwards. We must take the historical questions and challenges on board; we cannot retreat into a private world of "faith" which history cannot touch (what sort of a god would we be "believing" in if we did?). The forward direction may not be comfortable, either for scholarship or the church. Forward directions seldom are; and I do not say that with the glee of the scholar who sees that his own agenda will be uncomfortable *for everybody else,* though not for him. If there is discomfort here, I share it.

The Third Quest, then, is the basic starting-point of *Jesus and the Victory of God.* It correctly highlights Jewish eschatology as the key to understanding Jesus. By following up and sharpening its questions, and honing and using its methods, we can attain real advance in our understanding of Jesus within his historical context, and thus raise in new ways the vital questions of continuity and discontinuity between Jesus of Nazareth and

Christian faith—and between the *agenda* of Jesus of Nazareth and the contemporary *task* of the church. As we look at the history, we discover that we are also, and at the same time, looking at the traditional subject matter of Christian theology, and that such theology is not to be separated from Christian praxis. To put it the other way round: when the New Testament writers speak of their encounter with Jesus as an encounter with Israel's god, they are redefining what "god" (or even "God") means at least as much as they are redefining who Jesus was and is. The dichotomies between event and interpretation, between fact and value, are not ultimate, and it is precisely when we are studying Jesus that they break down in disarray (see Thatcher 1993). This relativizes some Third Quest work, to be sure, with its potential for materialist reductionism. But it hits far harder, as Schweitzer saw, at the anti-historical idealism of the iconographers on the one hand and the silhouette-makers on the other. To put it bluntly, we can know quite a lot about Jesus; not enough to write a modern-style biography, including the color of the subject's hair, and what he liked for breakfast, but quite a lot. What we know, with the kind of "knowledge" proper to all historical inquiry, may turn out to generate theological and practical significance far in excess of, and perhaps quite different from, anything that recent scholarship, and recent Christianity, has imagined or wanted. The renewed New Quest has sometimes implied that it and only it can make the study of Jesus relevant, at least to contemporary North America. I suggest that a far greater relevance will result from a more serious historical enterprise, although we cannot predict in advance what this relevance may be. As the first Christian century discovered, whole-hearted discipleship of Jesus by no means leads to unthinking support for the *status quo,* whether in religion or in politics.

Authentic Christianity, after all, has nothing to fear from history. Rather, scholars of all backgrounds now have the opportunity, given us not least by the massive wave of discoveries about and research into first-century Judaism, to answer the questions raised by Reimarus, Schweitzer, Bultmann, Sanders, Crossan and the others, and even perhaps those raised by Luther and Melanchthon. The opportunity is at hand to respond appropriately to the challenge of the Enlightenment, and in so doing to issue some counter-challenges from the perspective of a history that, however rigorous, has not abandoned theology, but has rather rediscovered theological possibilities hidden under the pile of icons or behind the stack of silhouettes. History, even if bedraggled from its sojourn in the far country, may yet come home to a celebration.

Abbreviations

ABD	*Anchor Bible Dictionary*
ABRL	Anchor Bible Reference Library
BibInt	*Biblical Interpretation*
ET	English Translation
FBBS	Facet Books–Biblical Series
Ign. *Rom.*	Ignatius, *To the Romans*
IRT	Issues in Religion and Theology
JTS	*Journal of Theological Studies*
LJS	Lives of Jesus Series
OBS	Oxford Bible Series
SBEC	Studies in the Bible and Early Christianity
SBT	Studies in Biblical Theology
SJT	*Scottish Journal of Theology*
SNTSU	Studien zum Neuen Testament in Seiner Umwelt
WUNT	Wissenschaftliche Untersuchungen zum Neuen Testament

Bibliography

Alexander, Philip S. 1992. "'The Parting of the Ways' from the Perspective of Rabbinic Judaism." In *Jews and Christians: The Parting of the Ways, A.D. 70 to 135,* edited by J. D. G. Dunn, 1–25. WUNT 66. Tübingen: Mohr/ Siebeck.

Bailey, Kenneth E. 1983. *Poet & Peasant and Through Peasant Eyes: A Literary-Cultural Approach to the Parables in Luke.* Grand Rapids: Eerdmans.

Bammel, Ernst, and C. F. D. Moule, editors. 1984. *Jesus and the Politics of His Day.* Cambridge: Cambridge Univ. Press.

Bauckham, Richard. 1992. "Jesus, Worship of." In *ABD* 3:812–19.

Betz, Otto. 1968. *What Do We Know about Jesus?* Translated by M. Kohl. London: SCM.

Borg, Marcus. 1984. *Conflict, Holiness and Politics in the Teaching of Jesus.* SBEC 5. New York: Mellen. (Reprinted by Harrisburg, Pa.: TPI, 1998.)

———. 1987a. *Jesus: A New Vision.* San Francisco: Harper & Row.

———. 1987b. "An Orthodoxy Reconsidered: The 'End-of-the-World Jesus.'" In *The Glory of Christ in the New Testament: Studies in Christology in Memory of George Bradford Caird,* edited by L. D. Hurst and N. T. Wright, 207–17. Oxford: Oxford Univ. Press.

———. 1994. *Meeting Jesus Again for the First Time: The Historical Jesus and the Heart of Contemporary Faith.* San Francisco: Harper-SanFrancisco.

Bornkamm, Günther. 1960. *Jesus of Nazareth.* Translated by I. McLusky, F. McLusky, and J. M. Robinson. New York: Harper.

Bowker, John. 1973. *Jesus and the Pharisees.* Cambridge: Cambridge Univ. Press.

Brandon, S. G. F. 1967. *Jesus and the Zealots: A Study of the Political Factor in Primitive Christianity.* Manchester: Manchester Univ. Press.

Brown, Colin. 1984. *Miracles and the Critical Mind.* Grand Rapids: Eerdmans.

———. 1988. *Jesus in European Protestant Thought: 1778–1860.* Grand Rapids: Baker.

Brown, Raymond E. 1994. *The Death of the Messiah: From Gethsemane to the Grave: A Commentary on the Passion Narratives in the Four Gospels.* New York: Doubleday.

Buchanan, George W. 1984. *Jesus: The King and His Kingdom.* Macon, Ga.: Mercer Univ. Press.

Bultmann, Rudolf. 1958. *Jesus and the Word.* New York: Scribner. (German ed. 1926.)

———. 1968. *The History of the Synoptic Tradition.* Rev. ed. Translated by J. Marsh. New York: Harper & Row. (3rd German ed. 1958.)

Caird, G. B. *The Gospel of St. Luke.* London: Penguin.

———. 1965. *Jesus and the Jewish Nation.* London: Athlone.

———. 1980. *The Language and Imagery of the Bible.* Philadelphia: Westminster.

———. 1982. "Jesus and Israel: The Starting Point for New Testament Christology." In *Christological Perspectives: Essays in Honor of Harvey K. McArthur,* edited by R. F. Berkey and S. Edwards, 58–68. New York: Pilgrim.

Charlesworth, James H. 1988. *Jesus within Judaism: New Light from Exciting Archaeological Discoveries.* New York: Doubleday.

Chilton, Bruce. 1979. *God in Strength: Jesus' Announcement of the Kingdom.* SNTSU B/1. Freistadt: Plöchl. (Reprinted by JSOT Press, 1987.)

———. 1984. *A Galilean Rabbi and His Bible.* Wilmington, Del.: Glazier.

———. 1992. *The Temple of Jesus: His Sacrificial Program within a Cultural History of Sacrifice.* University Park, Pa.: Pennsylvania State Univ. Press.

Crossan, John Dominic. 1991. *The Historical Jesus: The Life of a Mediterranean Jewish Peasant.* San Francisco: HarperSanFrancisco.

de Jong, Marius. 1991. *Jesus: The Servant-Messiah.* New Haven: Yale Univ. Press.

Derrett, J. D. M. 1973. *Jesus's Audience: The Social and Psychological Environment in Which He Worked.* New York: Seabury.

Dodd, C. H. 1961. *The Parables of the Kingdom.* Rev. ed. New York: Scribner.

————. 1971. *The Founder of Christianity.* New York: Macmillan.

Downing, John. 1963. "Jesus and Martyrdom." *JTS* 14:279–93.

Downing, F. Gerald. 1992. *Cynics and Christian Origins.* Edinburgh: T. & T. Clark.

————. 1995. "Words as Deeds and Deeds as Words." *BibInt* 3:129–43.

Dunn, James D. G. 1975. *Jesus and the Spirit: A Study of the Religious and Charismatic Experience of Jesus and the First Christians as Reflected in the New Testament.* Philadelphia: Westminster.

Epp, Eldon J., and George MacRae, editors. 1989. *The New Testament and Its Modern Interpreters.* The Bible and Its Modern Interpreters. Philadelphia: Fortress Press.

Farmer, William. 1956. *Maccabees, Zealots, and Josephus: An Inquiry into Jewish Nationalism in the Greco-Roman Period.* New York: Columbia Univ. Press.

————. 1982. *Jesus and the Gospel.* Philadelphia: Fortress Press.

Fredriksen, Paula. 1988. *From Jesus to Christ: The Origins of the New Testament Images of Jesus.* New Haven: Yale Univ. Press.

Freyne, Sean. 1988. *Galilee, Jesus and the Gospels: Literary Approaches and Historical Investigations.* Philadelphia: Fortress Press.

Glasson, T. F. 1984. "Schweitzer's Influence— Blessing or Bane?" In *The Kingdom of God,* edited by B. D. Chilton, 107–20. IRT. Philadelphia: Fortress Press. (Orig. art. 1977.)

Goergen, Donald. 1986a. "The Death and Resurrection of Jesus." In *A Theology of Jesus,* vol. 2. Wilmington, Del.: Glazier.

———. 1986b. *A Theology of Jesus*. Vol. 1: *The Mission and Ministry of Jesus*. Wilmington, Del.: Glazier.

Harvey, Anthony E. 1982. *Jesus and the Constraints of History*. Philadelphia: Westminster.

———. 1990. *Strenuous Commands: The Ethic of Jesus*. Philadelphia: Trinity Press International.

Hengel, Martin. 1971. *Was Jesus a Revolutionist?* Translated by W. Klassen. FBBS. Philadelphia: Fortress Press. (German ed. 1970.)

———. 1973. *Victory over Violence: Jesus and the Revolutionists*. Translated by D. E. Green. Philadelphia: Fortress Press. (German ed. 1968.)

———. 1981. *The Charismatic Leader and His Followers*. Translated by J. Greig. New York: Crossroad. (German ed. 1968.)

Horsley, Richard A. 1987. *Jesus and the Spiral of Violence: Popular Jewish Resistance in Roman Palestine*. San Francisco: Harper & Row. (Reprinted by Philadelphia: Fortress Press, 1993.)

———. "The Death of Jesus." In *Studying the Historical Jesus,* edited by B. Chilton and C. A. Evans, 395–422. Leiden: Brill.

Hurtado, Larry. 1988. *One God, One Lord: Early Christian Devotion and Ancient Jewish Monotheism*. Philadelphia: Fortress Press.

Jeremias, Joachim. 1958. *Jesus' Promise to the Nations*. Translated by S. H. Hooke. SBT 1/24. Naperville, Ill.: Allenson. (German ed. 1956.)

———. 1971. *New Testament Theology*. Vol. 1: *The Proclamation of Jesus*. Translated by J. Bowden. New York: Scribner.

Johnson, Luke Timothy. 1995. *The Real Jesus: The Misguided Quest for the Historical Jesus and the Truth of the Traditional Gospels.* San Francisco: HarperSanFrancisco.

Kähler, Martin. 1964. *The So-called Historical Jesus and the Historic, Biblical Christ.* Translated by C. Braaten. Philadelphia: Fortress Press. (German ed. 1892.)

Käsemann, Ernst. 1964. *Essays on New Testament Themes.* Translated by W. J. Montague. SBT 1/41. Naperville, Ill.: Allenson. (German ed. 1960; reprinted Philadelphia: Fortress Press, 1982.)

Klausner, Joseph. 1945. *Jesus of Nazareth: His Life, Times, and Teaching.* Translated by H. Danby. New York: Macmillan.

Leivestad, Ragnar. 1987. *Jesus in His Own Perspective: An Examination of His Sayings, Actions, and Eschatological Titles.* Minneapolis: Augsburg.

Lohfink, Gerhard. 1984. *Jesus and Community.* Translated by J. P. Galvin. Philadelphia: Fortress Press. (2nd German ed. 1982.)

Maccoby, Hyam. 1980. *Revolution in Judea: Jesus and the Jewish Resistance.* New York: Taplinger. (First published 1973.)

Mack, Burton L. 1988. *A Myth of Innocence: Mark and Christian Origins.* Philadelphia: Fortress Press.

Manson, T. W. 1953. *The Servant-Messiah: A Study of the Public Ministry of Jesus.* Cambridge: Cambridge Univ. Press.

McGrath, Alister E. 1994. *The Making of Modern German Christology, 1750–1990.* Grand Rapids: Zondervan. (1st ed. 1986.)

Meier, John. 1991. *A Marginal Jew: Rethinking the Historical Jesus*. Vol. 1: *The Roots of the Problem and the Person*. ABRL. New York: Doubleday.

———. 1994. *A Marginal Jew: Rethinking the Historical Jesus*. Vol. 2: *Mentor, Message, and Miracles*. ABRL. New York: Doubleday.

Melanchthon, Philipp. 1982. *Melanchthon on Christian Doctrine: Loci Communes 1555*, Edited and translated by C. L. Manschreck. Grand Rapids: Baker.

Meyer, Ben F. 1979. *The Aims of Jesus*. London: SCM.

———. 1992a. *Christus Faber: The Master-Builder and the House of God*. Allison Park, Pa.: Pickwick.

———. 1992b. "Jesus Christ." In *ABD* 3:773–96.

Morgan, Robert. 1987. "The Historical Jesus and the Theology of the New Testament." In *The Glory of Christ in the New Testament: Studies in Christology in Memory of George Bradford Caird*, edited by L. D. Hurst and N. T. Wright, 187–206. Oxford: Clarendon.

Moule, C. F. D. 1977. *The Origin of Christology*. Cambridge: Cambridge Univ. Press.

———. 1984. "Some Observations on *Tendenzkritik*." In Bammel and Moule 1984: 91–100.

Neill, Stephen C., and N. T. Wright. 1988. *The Interpretation of the New Testament, 1861–1986*. Oxford: Oxford Univ. Press.

Neusner, Jacob. 1993. *A Rabbi Talks with Jesus: An Intellectual, Interfaith Exchange*. New York: Doubleday.

Neyrey, Jerome H. 1991. "Preface." In *The Social World of Luke-Acts: Models for Interpretation*, edited by J. H. Neyrey, ix–xviii. Peabody, Mass.: Hendrickson.

Oakman, Douglas E. 1986. *Jesus and the Economic Questions of His Day.* SBEC 8. Lewiston, N.Y.: Mellen.

O'Collins, Gerald. 1995. *Christology: A Biblical, Historical, and Systematic Study of Jesus.* Oxford: Oxford Univ. Press.

O'Neill, John C. 1980. *Messiah: Six Lectures on the Ministry of Jesus.* Cambridge: Cochrane.

Reimarus, Hermann Samuel. 1970. *Fragments.* Translated by R. S. Fraser. Edited by C. H. Talbert. LJS. Philadelphia: Fortress Press. (German ed. 1778.)

Renan, Ernest.1863. *La Vie de Jésus.* Paris: Frères.

Ruether, Rosemary. 1974. *Faith and Fratricide: The Theological Roots of Anti-Semitism.* New York: Seabury.

Riches, John. 1980. *Jesus and the Transformation of Judaism.* London: Darton, Longman & Todd.

Riesner, Rainer. 1984. *Jesus als Lehrer: eine Untersuchung zum Ursprung der Evangelien-Überlieferung.* WUNT 2/7. Tübingen: Mohr/Siebeck. [1981]

Rivkin, Ellis. 1984. *What Crucified Jesus?* Nashville: Abingdon.

Sanders, E. P. 1985. *Jesus and Judaism.* Philadelphia: Fortress Press.

———. 1992. *Judaism: Practice and Belief, 63 BCE–66 CE.* Philadelphia: Trinity Press International.

———. 1993. *The Historical Figure of Jesus.* London: Penguin.

Schillebeeckx, Edward. 1979. *Jesus: An Experiment in Christology*. Translated by H. Hoskins. New York: Seabury. (Orig. ed. 1974.)

Schüssler Fiorenza, Elisabeth. 1983. *In Memory of Her: A Feminist Theological Reconstruction of Christian Origins*. New York: Crossroad.

———. 1994. *Jesus. Miriam's Child, Sophia's Prophet: Critical Issues in Feminist Christology*. New York: Continuum.

Schweitzer, Albert. 1954. *The Quest of the Historical Jesus: A Critical Study of its Progress from Reimarus to Wrede*. Translated by J. Montgomery. New York: Macmillan. (1st complete ed., based on the 2nd German ed., Minneapolis: Fortress Press, 2001.)

Segundo, J. L. 1985. *Jesus of Nazareth Yesterday and Today*. Vol. 2: *The Historical Jesus of the Synoptics*. Translated by J. Drury. Maryknoll, N.Y.: Orbis.

Stanton, Graham. 1989. *The Gospels and Jesus*. OBS. Oxford: Oxford Univ. Press.

Strauss, David Friedrich. 1972. *The Life of Jesus Critically Examined*. Translated by G. Eliot. LJS. Philadelphia: Fortress Press. (German ed. 1835–36).

Thatcher, Adrian. 1993. "Resurrection and Rationality." In *The Resurrection of Jesus Christ*, edited by Paul Avis, 171–86. London: Darton, Longman, and Todd.

Theissen, Gerd. 1987. *The Shadow of the Galilean: The Quest of the Historical Jesus in Narrative Form*. Translated by J. Bowden. Philadelphia: Fortress Press. (German ed. 1986.)

Vermes, Geza. 1973. *Jesus the Jew: A Historian's Reading of the Gospels*. Philadelphia: Fortress Press.

——. 1981. *The Gospel of Jesus the Jew.* Newcastle upon Tyne: Univ. of Newcastle.

——. 1983. *Jesus and the World of Judaism.* Philadelphia: Fortress Press.

——. 1993. *The Religion of Jesus the Jew.* Minneapolis: Fortress Press.

Witherington, Ben III. 1990. *The Christology of Jesus.* Minneapolis: Fortress Press.

——. 1994. *Jesus the Sage: The Pilgrimage of Wisdom.* Minneapolis: Fortress Press.

——. 1995. *The Jesus Quest: The Third Search for the Jew of Nazareth.* Downers Grove, Ill.: InterVarsity.

Wrede, William. 1971. *The Messianic Secret.* Translated by J. C. Grieg. Cambridge: Clarke.

Wright, N. T. 1986. "'Constraints' and the Jesus of History." *SJT* 39:189–210.

——. 1991. *The Climax of the Covenant: Christ and the Law in Pauline Theology.* Minneapolis: Fortress Press.

——. 1992a. *Christian Origins and the Question of God.* Vol. 1: *The New Testament and the People of God.* Minneapolis: Fortress Press.

——. 1992b. "Jesus, Quest for the Historical." In *ABD* 3:796–802.

——. 1996. *Christian Origins and the Question of God.* Vol. 2: *Jesus and the Victory of God.* Minneapolis: Fortress Press.

Yoder, John Howard. 1994. *The Politics of Jesus: Vicit Agnus Noster.* 2nd ed. Grand Rapids: Eerdmans. (1st ed. 1972.)

Zeitlin, Irving M. 1988. *Jesus and the Judaism of His Time.* Oxford: Blackwell.